The POWER *of* PRAYER

The POWER *of* PRAYER

CHUCKS UZONWANNE

To order additional copies of this book, contact:
Xlibris
0-800-056-3182
www.xlibrispublishing.co.uk
Orders@xlibrispublishing.co.uk
669596

CONTENTS

DEDICATION

For all those whose hearts are genuinely praying for peace in the world.

For all those whose hearts are genuinely praying for God's unity of purpose?

For all those who are supplicating for the down trodden and oppressed.

For all those who are interceding for sinners lost in the world.

For all those who are martyred preaching the gospel of Jesus Christ?

For all those who are genuinely praying for orphans, and all the widows in the world

This book is fondly dedicated to you all, and I pray that the power of prayer will mantle your hearts and minds to speak Spirit-filled, life transforming and dynamic words able to break asunder and destroy every yoke and shackle of the enemy and liberate the bound.

Chucks Uzonwanne

ENDORSEMENT

I t is through only under the influence and inspiration of a Divine guidance can a prevailing and potent biblical exegeses and revelations infuse into a study of prayer in order to bring home the essence behind Prayer. Which Pastor Chucks Uzonwanne successfully and arduously did in his book, The Power of Prayer. The Book gave an unmistakeably, undoubtedly, unquestionable and undiluted new meaning to prayer, which will in no diminutive measure facilitate to unwrap and stamp in the mind of people who have mishit, misunderstand and underestimate the essence of prayer, to correctively, efficiently and effectively use it as a mean through which God will establish His thought that means well for us and ready to accomplish our heart desires in line with his will and word.

The Book is so detailed and highly structured in that even atheist, non Christians and immature Christians can draw from its biblical encounters to understand clearly and precisely the importance of Prayer and Praying.

Pastor Chucks handed to those who want to make a change in their situations, to effect life and walk in the Spirit through prayer an immeasurable tool made available in The Power of Prayer.

Kenechukwu Chukwunwejim
Senior Pastor
Victory Christian Mission London.
Lecturer: Christ Universal Bible College London.

Pastor Chucks is one of God's Generals! His books have equipped the Saints to ascertain and accomplish their purpose in life. And his teaching has established himself one of God's great army of this end time.

Reading through this book, I thought to myself, "Pastor Chucks is one of the most well read Biblical minister I know." I could perceive the Biblical and Spiritual insights he is trying to communicate to people of God.

I enjoyed the fact that in his communication he discussed about Faith; one can actually hear him talk about God himself and what God can do when we put our faith into action. He did not leave out Jesus nor did he leave out the Holy Spirit. In the same manner, in his aligning and embedding faith into prayer; the Father, Son, and the Holy Spirit were equally embraced in the discussion.

In Pastor Chucks' revelation of wisdom, he elucidated the wisdom of man and the wisdom of the Holy Spirit. This book will not only be uncomplicated for a young Christian to read but also will be easily comprehensible for an unbeliever.

I will encourage every pastor to put this book in their church book store and also recommend it to members of their church.

I praise God Almighty for the wisdom of God on Pastor Chucks Uzonwanne in putting this down into a book. Bless you all as you read this book. Bless you, Man of God.

Pastor Ify Adimibe
Founder/ President
Living Water House International,
Islington/ Christian Centre Nigeria.

WORDS OF ENCOURAGEMENT
FROM PASTOR CHUCKS
BE MOTIVATED & TEACHABLE

"The insightful way to be successfully motivated, humble and teachable is through the power of prayer. This fervent and effectual praying helps you discover focus and perspective, humility and a true and intimate relationship with God. With this you can gain knowledge and stand immovable and irrefutably strong in the Lord. Be therefore motivated to hear God on a daily basis by praying and applying the word to your spirit so as to put on a teachable attitude wherever you go.

Encourage yourself to always pray and learn to be gentle and humble in your spirit, so you can hear the voice of the Spirit of the living God! This is because the quality of any relationship is determined by the quality of the communication. Which also reveals that it's not by force alone that man finds his reward but by prayer and supplication man's heart desire finds satisfaction in God."

"For you to effectively walk with God and intimately know him, you need the infusion of the power of prayer to make your life beautifully scented with the presence of God. Therefore, let the word of God gain mastery and be resident in your heart and spirit so you can always think positively to accomplish your destiny. This is because *a good heart is an open door for the Spirit of God to manifest.* This also infers that *you cannot fellowship with the Holy Spirit and remain the same neither can you effectively worship God unless you know him intimately and walk in his footsteps. Invariably, anyone who desires a relationship with God must be a person of prayer. Someone who has ears to listen to the voice of the Spirit of God, who is ready to surrender all else in order to gain Christ.*

This reveals that the purpose for which the scripture is given is not to help us earn a degree and increase our sense knowledge, but to change our lives. This also implies that the essence is for the word of God through prayer to:

- *Reform: To change from your old ways and improve your life by confessing Jesus Christ as your Lord and Saviour for all that pertain to life and godliness.*
- *Transform: A turning point that changes and converts you to be like Jesus.*
- *And conform: To become similar in harmony and act in accordance so as to put on the very image of him who created you.*

Therefore, prayerfully study and practice the bible to gain spiritual wisdom, insight into reality, so as to gain sound biblical knowledge for the transformation of your world by letting the word of God dwell richly in you as you propagate the gospel. It is the only armour and shield of faith needed to unleash the power of prayer if you're to stand successfully against the wiles of the devil."

ILLUMINATE YOUR WAY WITH PRAYER

"Never! Never! Never! Ever stop to pray; for in this dark world, prayer is the only light that will illuminate your way. So feed a soul with prayer and righteousness, and see a nation change. This is because righteousness exalts a nation and prayer preserves it. The heart that gives is the hand that receives, and prayer is the hand that brings to us the blessings which God has already provided."

BE INVOLVED

Our lifetime contains the only possibility required for every believer to play an active part in God's plan of salvation for humanity. Be committed and involved in the mission of saving the lost and help people reclaim their salvation in Christ Jesus by growing their faith through the study of the word and the power of prayer.

BE PURPOSEFUL

Being purposeful is making your life count for God; therefore be purposeful and fulfil your destiny in God. This is because as an ambassador of Christ, you cannot afford to forget your life assignment; for your destiny depends on it.

BE WORSHIPFUL

A thankful heart is the city of gratitude. Appreciate God with your worship and see grace open the door of your destiny.

Chucks Uzonwanne

SCRIPTURES FOR MEDITATION

'Our doubts are traitors, and make us lose the good we oft might win, by fearing to attempt.' William Shakespeare, Measure for Measure, 1604.

"The way of life is above to the wise, that he may depart from hell beneath" (Proverbs 15: 24).

"Be sober, be vigilant; because your adversary the devil, as a roaring lion, walketh about, seeking whom he may devour" (1 Peter 5: 8).

"Watch and pray that ye enter not into temptation" (Matthew 26: 41).

"Keep me as the apple of the eye, hide me under the shadow of thy wings" (Psalm 17: 8).

"Make thy face to shine upon thy servant: save me for thy mercies' sake" (Psalm 31: 16).

"He will keep the feet of his saints, and the wicked shall be silent in darkness; for by strength shall no man prevail" (1 Samuel 2: 9).

PRAYER OF MEDITATION & BLESSING

"Peace I leave with you, my peace I give unto you: not as the world giveth, give I unto you. Let not your heart be troubled, neither let it be afraid" (John 14: 27).

"Thou wilt keep him in perfect peace, whose mind is stayed on thee: because he trusteth in thee" (Isaiah 26: 3).

"[22]And the LORD spake unto Moses, saying, [23]Speak unto Aaron and unto his sons, saying, On this wise ye shall bless the children of Israel, saying unto them, [24]The LORD bless thee, and keep thee: [25]The LORD make his face shine upon thee, and be gracious unto thee: [26]The LORD lift up his countenance upon thee, and give thee peace. [27]And they shall put my name upon the children of Israel; and I will bless them" (Numbers 6: 22 – 27).

FOREWORD

The credibility in the perfect attempt to bring out the richness in the power of prayer is a laudable inspiration. The Power of Prayer serves as a wakeup call to all believers who desire the ability to pray effectively. This book will inspire in you the hunger to pray in a manner sure to awaken that dormant, intrinsic ability, and will also enhance your knowledge to pray with results. This makes the power of prayer insightful and innately able to teach you how to pray the right way by you confessing the truth of God's word and watching it bring transformation that will arouse the giant in you to pray always. This indeed is proving positive that *"Prayer ascends by fire, and flame gives prayer access as well as wings, acceptance as well as energy. There is no incense without fire, no prayer without flame."*

PREFACE

The step by step trilogy of prayer mastered in the power of prayer is a revelation that will bring transformation to the hungry soul. The power of prayer is crafted in such a way that your faith impacts your belief to get whatever you're asking for with such impunity that reveals confidence in the power that is in the word of God. These trilogies of prayer; ask, belief and faith are needed vehicles able to bring reformation and change every seen and unforeseen circumstance.

When you think of power, ability or authority and contemplate prayer; asking, believing and receiving in faith you'll see the fusion of this trilogy that's in the power of prayer. It will energise, activate and transport you to a realm beyond human comprehension, and bring you revelations of the spirit able to surmount every inhibition of darkness.

The power of prayer is an expose of light that will shine forth spiritual verities able to unveil scales of obscurity beclouding your journey to higher life. This is because it is endued with ability to enact ultimate intimacy with Almighty Jehovah, with perspective and fervour to stay your mind always on prayer so you can find perfect peace in Christ Jesus.

INTRODUCTION

The importance attached to the inspiration which the power of prayer creates is the inundation with the ability to pray, and the insight it grants you to conceive thoughts that are true. This will make you believe for your faith to be active and will enhance your relationship and confidence in God. The power of prayer will also cause you to bear the fruits of righteousness and make you operate in the gifts of the Spirit as you delve into the realms of the spirit through prayer and the study of the word of God. These are befitting description of the intimacy you are about to inherit from the power of prayer. You will discover they paint the picture of what the fruits of prayer can do in your life; and the essence is to lead, guide and introduce you to how they can be yours when you put them to regular practice. This will cause you to acquire that intrinsic ability that exists as a natural and integral part of you once you obey and do what the word of God says. Also, it will reveal the importance of the power of this ability called 'prayer' and unveil for you the things you need to do to awaken, develop and harness your prayer life. All of these will cause you to be spiritually stalwart, able to use the power of prayer advantageously to the full.

To reiterate there is power in prayer is no gainsaying! So, get ready; for the power of prayer will challenge you to hear, heed and do the word for results. And also convert and metamorphose you to be humble, teachable and obedient to the voice of the Spirit of God. Furthermore, it will invite you to reflect, introspect and retrospect on what you want to make out of life. And also serve as a guide to lead and make you think, project and have perspective.

Above all, the power of prayer will always inspire you to get beside yourself with prayer and help to build your faith substantially.

To your advantage, the power of prayer will keep you hungry to pray regularly, and make you overcome your limits in life. Conversely, it will open for you a new door of faith that will spur your belief and make your walk with God a reality.

The power of prayer will make you learn and discover new spiritual terrains and things about yourself that will position you for greatness and success, giving you a new lease of life as you navigate your way through spiritual verities. This will open your eyes to your prayer-ability, your environment, people and society at large, in that, it will help you make an informed decision for higher meaningful life. It will enhance your horizon giving you an overview of the importance of prayer, and things perhaps that you didn't think were important to enhance your prayer life will be easily comprehensible. This will insightfully put you on the pedestal of grace to pray more effectively, having knowledge and experiencing the power of prayer at work in you.

Through the power of prayer you would learn and develop your faith to overcome unwanted habits and challenges that has made you complacent and resigned to status-quo. It will make you able to put past failures behind by using these seeming disadvantages as a spring board to higher realms of new discovery that will help your ability to positively stand your ground rooted in the word of God, and live your life by the dictates of the Spirit to the full. In conclusion, the power of prayer builds on practical Christian living.

- It reinforces the key points of our Christian faith and takes you on a revelatory journey of applying your faith through unwound stories of the Bible, causing you to believe the word of God irrefutably and effectively pray for results.

- It relates directly to the reality of life both past, present and in the future, and how it can be applied to your work life, social life and home life to bring about a positive change.

With these revelations accruing to your advantage as you pray and practice the word of God, it becomes imperative that the power of prayer will allow you dispel negative thoughts and build a catalyst that will establish your faith and define your walk with God. Further to the advantages of the power of prayer is that whatever level you are in, this everyday living practical tool looks in more details at how you are to come to terms with the bumps [setbacks] of life that trail your path. And how to achieve a solution to these life issues by rightly applying the word of God through the power of prayer. Also, the power of prayer will help you to discover your true self as you accomplish your purpose and are fulfilled in life by walking in your destiny to the glory of God.

CHAPTER ONE

THE POWER OF PRAYER

What is Prayer?

P rayer is a cultivated, developed and an intimate relationship with God for our benefit which makes God intercede on our behalf to do what he has promised. This makes prayer the key in the hand of faith that opens the door of destiny. This is because prayer gives the believer access into God's throne room and brings him into God's set time. This is the reason prayer is the hand that brings to us the blessings which God has already provided. This means that prayer is a walk with God? It is a relationship asking God to lead while we follow. Prayer therefore is petition, request, demand, plea, appeal or entreaty. It is an application to God in the form of words or thoughts which in return engender expectations from the applicator in response to answered prayer. In other words, prayer makes your believed expectation a reality when applied in faith because it is predicated on God's promises. This makes prayer a two-way communion.

"7Ask and it shall be given you; seek, and you shall find; knock and it shall be opened unto you: 8For everyone that asketh receiveth; and he that seeketh findeth; and to him that knocketh it shall be opened" (Matthew 7: 7-8).

"Be careful for nothing; but in everything by prayer and supplication with thanksgiving let your requests be made known unto God. And the peace of God, which passeth all understanding, shall keep your hearts and minds through Christ Jesus" (Philippians 4: 6 - 7).

Prayer entails asking, seeking, knocking, meditation, listening, obedience, agreement, intercession, and thanksgiving. Where all avenues have been explored and every sense of reason exhausted, prayer is what the believer needs to keep standing because it will spur him to go the extra mile. This implies that he must believe a change is inevitable for there to be a change regardless of time, season and opposition. This is because prayer inter-relates with faith and believing. They inter-depend and are mutually connected to asking. These reasons being that before you can effectively pray there are factors that determine the value of this attached importance in the sense that prayer deals with desires that stem from want and needs, and also the hunger to establish an intimate relationship with God; the benevolent source of providence who meets all need. The fact that you use prayer as a means to accomplish these purposes explains:

- On your own you can do nothing. It is not by power nor is it by might, but by God's Spirit.
- That you desire for God to guide and lead you shows he's your Shepherd and the Way.
- For you to accomplish these purposes on your own is beyond your control to effect a change.
- You are looking up to a higher and superior being for intervention. He is all-knowing.
- The one whom you're praying to is more than able to provide the object of your desire and change hopeless situations in your life because all power belongs to him.

CHUCKS UZONWANNE

- He determines what you get and when it will be best suitable. He is your pre-designator.
- He has knowledge of why you're asking or praying because He knows the end of the matter from the beginning.
- He identifies with you and wants you to have the very best. He is your source.
- The intent of your heart is the determinant for measuring God's perfect will for you. This means that your understanding of God's perfect will helps your decision making, for your heart desire to be in sync with the promises of God when you pray. This further means your request will be determined by the understanding of the things your thoughts conceived as your prayer need, measured at the backdrop of God's perfect will for you. With such clarity, the receipt of your request will be absolute and certain. This infers that every seed you sow is what comes back to you because God responds to your desire or conceived thoughts based on the values of your prayer request.

All of these must be predicated at the backdrop of you 'believing' when you pray. You must believe that the one to whom you're praying hears and is willing not only to answer but also able to meet your requests because it is in consonance to his will. In this case, that your confidence rests on the ores of God's perfect will indirectly suggests that as you pray, you are calling forth into existence the power of creation to infuse the object of your desire. However, for this to become a reality; you need 'faith.' You need faith to please the one to whom you're asking from. You need faith to believe in the one you're asking from. And you need faith to receive the object of your desire from he who is able to do exceeding abundantly above all that you may ask or think according to his mighty power which is at work in you.

THE ESSENCE OF FAITH

Faith creates an atmosphere for spiritual verities that enables you to see with the eyes of the spirit the reality of what you're asking for before it becomes yours tangibly. This implied essence means there is a condition for receiving which must be predicated on faith when you pray which the Bible sums up in the following scriptures:

> "*⁶But without faith it is impossible to please him [God]: for he that cometh to God must believe that he is, and that he is a rewarder of them that diligently seek him... ¹³These all died in faith... having seen them afar off, and were persuaded of them, and embraced them, and confessed...*" (Hebrews 11: 6 & 13).
>
> "*²²And Jesus answering saith unto them, Have faith in God. ²³For verily I say unto you, That whosoever shall say unto this mountain, Be thou removed, and be thou cast into the sea; and shall not doubt in his heart, but shall believe that those things which he saith shall come to pass; he shall have whatsoever he saith. ²⁴Therefore I say unto you, What things so ever ye desire, when ye pray, believe that ye receive them, and ye shall have them*" (Mark 11: 22-24).

These previewed scriptures reveal the paramount importance of faith in our relationship with God without which we cannot please him. This means that faith is the determinant to receiving [a request] from God. It also reveals that faith is something we can only see with the eyes of the spirit, confess with our mouth for possession and accept as reality. This also infers that faith is resolute and consequent on the word of God regardless of circumstances. This answers to why our Lord Jesus Christ in admonishing emphasised the need to have the God kind of faith, revealing that God himself is faith-God which is responsible for the reason he calls forth things that be not as though they already are in existence. This further reveals the immutability of God in the sense that he cannot be inhibited or limited by circumstances because he does not see impossibility whenever he desires for creation or for his thoughts to manifest. Furthermore, this explains the summary of Jesus' statement that *if you shall believe with your heart and say with your mouth by faith to this mountain [of impossibility, doubt, sickness, disease, infirmity, lack, poverty, hatred, disappointments, confusion, failure, barrenness, oppression, anger, etc] be removed and cast into the sea [of oblivion so you can receive a renewed life], confessing without doubting in your heart but believing in those things which you have decreed and spoken into the air; the arena of the spirit of life, you will have them.* He concludes by exposing reassuringly that for your desire to manifest, you need 'prayer'; for your prayer to become a reality, you need 'believe'; for you to receive the tangibility of your reality, you need 'faith.'

PRAYER EXERCISE

1. What is prayer?
Prayer is a cultivated, developed and an intimate
relationship with God for benefit which makes God intercede
on our behalf to do that which he has promised.

2. How can you have faith when you pray?
By believing in the promises of God

3. Why must a believer pray? See page 30 - 31

_____

_____

_____

4. What are the things you need for your
desire to manifest? See pages 29 - 33

_____

_____

_____

CHUCKS UZONWANNE

CHAPTER TWO

HOW TO PRAY

LETTER TO MY FATHER

Dear Heavenly Father,

I ask for your grace to do uncommon things today, and be the vessel that you use to make things happen on earth that will bring you glory and be a blessing to all mankind. It is my desire according to your injunctions to see the sinner saved, the sick receive their healing and the poor comforted with the good news of the love of our Lord and Saviour Jesus Christ. I pray that your word will always be in my heart and in my mouth as I proclaim your love, revealing who you are to nations of the world so they may know you in truth and fellowship with you in spirit. Father, I thank you for hearing and answering me in the mighty name of our Lord Jesus Christ, amen.

PRAYER FOR YOU!

As I embark on the journey of the prayer of faith, I pray that from above the power of prayer will mantle me for an upward and higher life, and grant me revelation knowledge that I may do exploits in his name.

I pray that the power of prayer makes me to be insightful with spiritual wisdom and grants me sound mind, causing the eyes of my understanding to be enlightened that I may see beyond the optical and know the hope of my calling in Christ Jesus.

I pray in the name of Jesus that the power of prayer be a reliable companion to keep me astute, focused in perspective and be an invaluable resource for my walk with God as I bring him glory and honour in my entire endeavour in Jesus mighty name, Amen.

PRAYER FOR YOU!

Father, I thank you for as I read this book and study in the name of Jesus, the eyes of my understanding are enlightened with spiritual wisdom, and revelation knowledge granted to me that I may know the hope of my calling.

I thank you Oh Lord God that by the agency of your holy presence your word gains residency and mastery in my spirit, reforming and transforming me that I may conform to reflect your image and be in your likeness.

I confess that my life is for your glory and honour as I walk in victory and in dominion, in strength and in divine health. I receive sound mind and grace for increase in every area of my life.

Holy Spirit, I adore you for refreshing me with your living word and inundating me with your grace that I may shine forth your glory, finding favour with men, being fruitful and productive in all my endeavours.

Father, I thank and bless you and give you all the glory for hearing and answering my prayer in the name of Jesus! Amen.

PRAYER OF PROPHECY FOR YOU!

In the name of Jesus, I speak forth and invoke words with the dynamic ability to recreate destinies into your life. I see God's prophetic predestination agenda concerning you unfold as I pray that the purposes of God for your life take root this instance and begin to manifest all that pertain to life and godliness to the glory of God.

May he who has called you with grace bless the work of your hands and increase you always to find fulfilment as you discover your destiny through the power of prayer.

May the dew of heaven rest upon you and cause where the souls of your feet threads upon to yield its increase to you as you continue to live perpetually and permanently under open heaven?

As a child of destiny, may your life always be upwards to reflect God's glory and ignite your soul with his Holy Presence to do exploit in his name.

And as you study and meditate regularly on the word of God; may the grace of God mantle you always to find favour with all men as you have found favour with God.

And may the light of God's countenance shine providence upon you and cause you to receive the gentle touch of God to run the race of life being fulfilled and walking in your destiny to his glory in the name of Jesus, amen.

PRAYER OF BLESSING

Father, I thank you for blessing this day in the life of your people.

A great day of blessing that will bring a change in someone's destiny!

In the name of Jesus, I see the door of your destiny opened by the power of the Most High God! And God's outpouring blessings flowing into your destiny and estranging every depravity and unwanted things, bringing healing to your spirit, your soul, your body and in every area of your life.

I decree God's blessings to bridge every gap in your destiny, and position you for greatness and for success, causing you to walk in victory and dominion, in divine health and in strength.

Father I thank you, for those who through faith believe in your blessing that their needs are met. May the outpouring of your blessing be for the healing of their destiny as your word take root in their spirit, shining forth the light of your righteousness to protect, guide and lead them by your Spirit to accomplish their purpose and walk in their destiny?

Thank you Father for they will continually walk in victory and in dominion, in strength and in divine health.

Thank you King of glory, Lord of all the earth for you have granted their request and met all their needs by the outpouring of your grace, in the mighty name of our Lord Jesus Christ. Amen.

PRAYER OF CONFESSION

I confess that I'm a child of God, born of his Spirit. The Life of God is at work in every fibre of my being. I confess that I'm blessed because God has made all favour and earthly blessings mine in abundance. I am sufficiently blessed because God has pronounced me blessed. I believe and receive from God that I'm graced with abundant blessings to be fulfilled in all my endeavours and be a blessing to my world, bearing the fruit of righteousness always.

I am blessed and a blessing because lack and poverty are estranged in my life. Sickness, infirmity and diseases have been cut off from my generations and are far from me; joy and strength are my standing in Christ Jesus as I put on the garment of praise to my God.

Because I am blessed, the doors of my destiny are opened unto me in victory and in dominion, in greatness and in success. Therefore, I confess that I will always walk and not stumble and will run and not grow weary because the joy of the Lord is always my strength.

Because I am blessed, every situation seen and unseen, known and unknown are working together for my good. Because I am blessed, God has made all grace to abound unto me so I will always in all circumstances be sufficiently furnished unto every good work in the mighty name of our Lord and Saviour Jesus Christ, amen.

PRAYER FOR DAILY LIVING

Here and now, I pray that the Lord God before whom I walk send his angel to guide me and prosper my way. In the name of Jesus Christ, may my aroma be as the smell of a field which the Lord God has blessed? May God give me the dew of heaven and the fatness of the earth that I may have plenty of corn and wine?

May God Almighty bless and make the work of my hands to be fruitful and productive. May he multiply me and cause me to be a multitude of people. And give me the blessing of Abraham and cause me to inherit the land wherein the soul of my feet treads upon. May people serve me and let nations bow down to me. Because I am blessed, cursed is everyone that curses me, and blessed is he that blesses me. Whosoever blesses me shall receive abundance of blessings.

Behold, I am with you, says the Lord, and will keep you wherever you go. I will not leave you until I have fulfilled my word in you. Your seed shall be as the dust of the earth and you will spread abroad to the west, and to the east, and to the north, and to the south, carrying the light of God's righteousness to the ends of the world; preaching and teaching the truth of God's word and his love to all nations in the name of Jesus Christ. Amen.

PRAYER OF IMPARTATION

Father, I thank you for your banner over me is love!

Holy Spirit, I welcome you as I stir the water of the Spirit of your word, creating atmosphere of miracles to inundate my spirit, soul and body and bring healing to my world.

I pray Oh God that your word will mantle my heart and mind to think the right thoughts always leading me to witness the gospel of our Lord Jesus Christ as I walk in your favour dominating and bringing you victory in all endeavours.

Holy Spirit, I thank you for enduing me with power and refreshing me with strength as I sit at thy feet to be taught and instructed in the way of your righteousness. I receive all that pertain to life and godliness with which to actively function and do great and uncommon things unto the glory of God the Father in the mighty name of our Lord Jesus Christ. Amen.

PRAYER OF ENLIGHTENMENT

Father, I thank you for enduing me with the power of insight and enlightenment!

Holy Spirit, I adore you for refreshing and inundating me with your glorious presence.

Lord Jesus, I thank you for access in your name, and for anointing me to receive the Spirit of your word into my heart and mind with which to do great exploit.

Lord God, as I study by your Spirit, I pray that your word will gain ascendancy in my spirit to bring transformation that will edify my spirit to conform and know you and the power of your resurrection.

Thank you for the entrance of your word brings the light that grants me spiritual wisdom, revelation knowledge, and enlightens the eyes of my understanding to bear the fruit of righteousness that causes me to always be fruitful and productive. Therefore, I decree that soundness of mind belongs to me, strength, divine health and grace for increase are mine, inundating every area of my life for success and greatness in the mighty name of our Lord Jesus Christ. Amen.

CHUCKS UZONWANNE

PRAYER OF UNITY

Father, as we gather in your Holy name, may your Holy Spirit's presence work within us. In the name of Jesus, make our gathering definitive and of unity of purpose. We pray Oh Lord God that as we sit at thy feet to be taught and instructed in righteousness that we be counselled on the inside and spiritually imparted. Our hearts and minds knitted as one; may be open to receive the Spirit and the truth of your word of life to propagate effectively the gospel of our Lord Jesus Christ.

Dear Lord God we thank you for illuminating our hearts and minds with spiritual verities as we receive knowledge and understanding. For granting us sound mind to assimilate and retain your living word in our spirit enabling us to dissect the word of truth for the impartation and transformation of our world with the Spirit of your holy word in the mighty name of our Lord Jesus Christ, Amen.

CHAPTER THREE

THE MIRACLE OF LIFE

"...but the gift of God is eternal life through Jesus Christ our Lord..."
(Romans 6: 23)

Life is a miracle! The miracle of life is simply the gift of God. It is a gift of the love of God to all humanity, and the beauty of it all is the enjoinment to do the will of God here on earth, so we can spend eternity with God through Christ Jesus. Humanity is forewarned so no one can say they never had the opportunity to partake of the grace and receive of this free gift of God.

The above preview reveals how we can accomplish eternity with God while on earth, ready for heaven. And makes us to understand that this gift of God is life without an end, and this life without an end is everlasting life that can only be found in God through Christ Jesus.

> *"Jesus saith unto him, I am the way, the truth, and the life: no man cometh unto the Father, but by me" (John 14: 6).*

I often ask; if you discover this gift of God in your life, which I believe some already have, *what would you do with it? How are you to appreciate the love of God for endowing you with his gifts and making you a blessing to your world? Would you in obedience prayerfully proclaim his love to your sphere of contact and to all mankind or are you one of those who don't care about the word of God or where you would spend eternity? Are you one of those who take the things of God for levity by saying there is no God, heaven or hell and do not see the relevance of prayer?*

I weep for all those whose opinion is born of ignorance! Those who ignorantly say there's no God, heaven or hell. There's need that you pay attention as I relate my experience with the manager of a bank I went to see. As we got talking, he asked me what I do for a living; and I told him I am a minister of the gospel of Christ, and the senior pastor of Christ House of Destiny Ministries. In continuance, I said that I'm also an author who writes books on how to have a relationship with God, exercise your faith and pray. There and then, I brought out two of my recently published books; my debut and best seller titled: **Faith for Increase: How to exercise your faith** and the second book titled: **Having Confidence in God Being Led by His Spirit**, and handed them over to him. He took them from me in appreciation and looked them over; admiring the art work cover page and the print quality up until when he read through the titles, and said, 'they were not for him.' In quick response, I said, *'How come?'* these are good books on how to exercise your faith and how to maintain an intimate relationship with God and have confidence in Him and be led by his Spirit. As though I was about to convince him to change his mind on his opinion, he quickly interjected and said, 'He is not a believer in anything.' That religion has never been his forte or a thing of concern to him, and therefore, lives his life as he deems fit. I was taken aback with a question on my mind, and immediately said, "You mean you don't believe in anything; not even, in the existence of God?"

Then he retorted and said, 'I believe there is a Supreme Being all right, but just can't be bothered with him or religion.' Further to my surprise at him for his ignorance was deducibly that he's such an intelligent gentle man. Then I asked him if he's not concerned about where he would spend eternity. In his own words, he said, 'When I die; then I'm dead, and that's case closed.' He concluded by saying that he wants to live his life without inhibitions or manmade rules and regulations, and nothing can persuade him to change his mind, not even God himself can convince him to believe in anything. I smiled and thought to myself, 'what an irony; 'manmade rules indeed' and you're working for one.'

Do you know many are like that; they can't be bothered and don't see the need to save their own souls from this untoward generation that's passing away into hell. Having concluded my transaction with him, I left his office convinced that I had deposited something that would make him have a rethink on his relationship with his maker and where he would spend eternity. And I also prayed for God to have mercy on him; convinced he doesn't know what he's saying. For these reasons, I pray oh Lord, for all those who can't be bothered with you and eternity because of their frivolous living. For all those who're too busy amassing wealth, and all those who spend their lives addicted to all sorts of influence. I pray that those swayed by unnecessary distractions may be convicted by the power of your Holy Spirit to seek and have intimate relationship with you oh God, in the mighty name of our Lord Jesus Christ. Amen.

Listen to what the Bible says, I believe it will help you make an informed decision to seek God while he may be found.

> "*3 But if our gospel be hid, it is hid to them that are lost: *4 In whom the god of this world hath blinded the minds of them which believe not, lest the light of the glorious gospel of Christ, who is the image of God, should shine unto them. *5 For we preach not ourselves, but Christ Jesus the Lord..."* (2 Corinthians 4: 3-5).*

> "*1 But of the times and the seasons, brethren, ye have no need that I write unto you. *2 For yourselves know perfectly*

CHUCKS UZONWANNE

that the day of the Lord so cometh as a thief in the night.
³For when they shall say, Peace and safety; then sudden
destruction cometh upon them, as travail upon a woman
with child; and they shall not escape. ⁴But ye, brethren,
are not in darkness, that that day should overtake you as a
thief. ⁵Ye are all the children of light, and the children of
the day: we are not of the night, nor of darkness. ⁶Therefore
let us not sleep, as do others; but let us watch and be sober.
⁷For they that sleep sleep in the night; and they that be
drunken are drunken in the night. ⁸But let us, who are
of the day, be sober, putting on the breastplate of faith
and love; and for an helmet, the hope of salvation" (1
Thessalonians 5: 1-8).

Beware my brethren, and know it's the god of this world system of technology, glamour, civilisation, get rich quick and bling-bling that has blinded the minds of those which believe not the glorious gospel of our Lord and Saviour Jesus Christ. These powers of darkness know that the day of the Lord cometh with God's judgment. So beware, many who once stood where you're standing now are gnashing their teeth in the lake of fire singing 'if I had known to heed the voice of reason and given my heart to the Lord.'

DISCOVERING YOUR TRUE SELF

You need to understand that the long suffering of God is an opportunity for anyone and all humanity to change and be reconciled to him. This will help you to receive salvation and know who you are and the purpose for your existence.

Have you ever asked yourself, *what is the essence for living? Is it so you can live as you please and throw caution to the wind?* Dearly beloved, you do not exist just so you can have a good job, be a successful business man or woman, chase after money and materiel things of the world, be a philanthropist, get married, have children, and grow old and die. No, you are more than that; you are born into this world majorly for two reasons which are: Service to God and service to all humanity. You're born to make a positive difference by making your life reflect the glory of God on earth and be a blessing to all humanity. Don't be like the bank manager or some of those who don't care about eternity. Eternity is real and discovering your true self in Christ and giving your heart to him will help you to fulfil the purposes of God in your life here on earth. This makes you a ready candidate for heaven. This is your passport and entry visa into the kingdom of God for that experience of eternal bliss in heaven.

How can you discover yourself? Discovering yourself is having an understanding of who God is and what he has called you to do through your gifts and calling that can only manifest after receiving salvation. The question now is *'do you know who you are?'* The prerequisite to knowing who you are is to be born again. This is the first step to discovering yourself.

For you to discover yourself means understanding there's the purposes of God deposited on the inside of you that makes you unique. This uniqueness lurking in you is what you need to discover and unveil the service of humanity to the glory of God. That is why you have not been consumed as a result of the grace of God, which indicates another opportunity for each day that you live to give your heart to God because he loves you and want your gifts to count. The reason is so you can be a blessing to your world because in you are the seed of greatness, the treasure of life. This seed of greatness is the voice of God that is waiting to seek expression through you to your world, only if you will let him. Understanding that you're a special seed makes you a good seed! You're a seed, not just a good seed but a destiny seed predestined for greatness. Therefore, don't fall by the way side, neither allow yourself to fall on arid and stony places, nor should you fall among thorns. For all the reasons in the world; fall on good ground and bring forth manifold fruits, so you can multiply to the blessing of the world. Wherefore, I need you to remember that our study scripture for this chapter in Romans 6: 23 makes us to understand that the phrase *'the gift of God'* is referring to our Lord Jesus Christ as the gift from God for our redemption. Jesus Christ is the grace for the salvation of all mankind who came to show the way for all to be reinstated and regain eternity through his atoned shed blood on Calvary cross. This was his assignment on earth; the very reason for you to discover your own assignment and make a difference to your world.

Jesus is that door through whom all mankind gains entrance into eternity with the Father. He knew his purpose and carried it to the latter. This is the reason for the grace and glory of God in your own life.

> *"Jesus saith unto him, I am the way, the truth, and the life: no man cometh unto the Father, but by me" (John 14: 6).*

The reason you have salvation is because Jesus paid the ultimate price with his life for your sake. He shed his precious uncontaminated with sin blood on the cross of Calvary so you might be reconciled to God.

Listen to this revelation, "Anyone and everyone who receives Jesus Christ and does the will of God, acknowledging him as their Lord and Saviour no matter what their sin nature or offences were will never die and go to hell, because they have received everlasting life in Christ Jesus."

> *"For God so loved the world, that he gave his only begotten Son, that whosoever believeth in him should not perish, but have everlasting life" (John 3: 16).*

> *"And this is the record, that God hath given to us eternal life, and this life is in his Son"(1 John 5: 11; see also John 5: 21-29).*

This is why the gift of God is eternal life through Christ Jesus our Lord. *Can you now see why you cannot afford to fail in fulfilling your destiny?* This is because there is so much vested in you by the One who has written and authored you for greatness and for success. He believes in you to the extent that he paid the ultimate price with his blood, so you can walk free, be fulfilled in your aspirations and destiny and live in eternity with him. This is his desire for you!

> *"And from Jesus Christ, who is the faithful witness...*
> *Unto him that loved us, and washed us from our sins in*
> *his own blood" (Revelation 1: 5).*

The phrases eternal life, everlasting life and life without an end connotes same meaning and will be used interchangeably. This means having an endless life with God in the hereafter through Jesus Christ. Jesus is the faithful witness from God who loves humanity and has washed as many as believe in him with his own blood for their redemption preparatory for eternal life. This also means that there is no other name wherein we can be saved and have this endless life but for the name of Jesus.

> *"Salvation is found in no one else, for there is no other*
> *name under heaven given to men by which we must be*
> *saved" (Acts 4: 12; see also Romans 6: 23).*

> *"And [Jesus] being found in fashion as a man, he*
> *humbled himself, and became obedient unto death, even*
> *the death of the cross"(Philippians 2: 8).*

The bible is clear on the reality of who Jesus is, and entreats that until you have discovered yourself in Jesus who was found in fashion as a man; humbled himself and became obedient unto God and died on the cross so you can have eternal life and make heaven, you cannot be free from eternal condemnation in hell.

CHUCKS UZONWANNE

Tell me, are you prepared for eternity or you are yet not sure? Have you resolved where you would spend eternity, heaven or hell? The Bible says:

> *"*[19]*I call heaven and earth to record this day against you, that I have set before you life and death, blessing and cursing: therefore choose life, that both thou and thy seed may live:* [20]*That thou mayest love the LORD thy God, and that thou mayest obey his voice, and that thou mayest cleave unto him: for he is thy life, and the length of thy days..." (Deuteronomy 30: 19-20).*

There is the witnessing of heaven and earth this day against all humanity according to the word of God that if they choose death, then they'd all be damned in hell. But, if they choose life the blessing of God will take root both in them and in all their seed, and grant them life here on earth and in eternity. This leaves everyone that passes through earth with choices. The choice you make today will determine your sojourning on earth and in eternity tomorrow. It's either you live for the glory of God here on earth by choosing life and walking in obedience to his word in righteousness or you follow the ways of the world that leads to death and destruction in hell. It is your decision to make, but know and realise that your redemption is within you and your day of salvation is now!

> If you will, *"confess with your mouth the Lord Jesus and believe in your heart that God has raised him from the dead [for your sake], you will be saved [from destruction and a life in hell]" (Romans 10: 9-10) Emphasis mine.*

> *"Whosoever shall confess that Jesus is the Son of God, God dwelleth in him, and he in God"(1 John 4: 15).*

CHAPTER FOUR

THE GIFT OF GOD

When we're not ashamed of the gospel of Christ, tremendous power of God unto salvation is made available to the believer. This is because the righteousness of God reveals the strength of our faith and helps us grow thereby. This explains the need for the believer who's justified of God to live by faith (Romans 1: 16 - 17). In other words, our Lord Jesus was delivered to die for our offences, and was raised from the dead for our justification (see 2 Corinthians 5: 21; Romans 4: 24 - 25 & Acts 2: 24). This means we have been justified by faith and are reconciled to God through our Lord Jesus Christ by whom we have access to grace that enables us to stand before God acquitted and to rejoice in the hope of his glory (Romans 5: 1 - 2).

Confessing the Lordship of Jesus and being baptized in his name is the only grace that's needed to receive salvation and the impartation of the gift of eternal life. This will help to clothe you with the glory of God and enable you to walk in victory and in dominion over every power of the enemy and also position you as candidate of heaven. This redemptive life is only made available to all without reservation through Christ Jesus, and can only be received when you confess and believe Jesus Christ to be your lord and saviour (see Romans 10: 9 -10 & Matthew 10: 32 - 33). One more thing however, the minute you confess and receive Jesus into your heart as your Lord and Saviour, your resolve must be to go and sin no more. The reason being that anyone who is born of God does not sin because the light of God's righteousness that has gained residency in him will not give place for darkness to thrive anymore. Therefore, if you will let the new life you've received flood your heart with God's light of redemption; it will lead and guide you to your destiny. And will open a new door of intimacy between you and your maker, which will bring transformation into your life. This is the reason the Bible says *to "arise and shine for your light has come and the glory of the Lord is risen upon you" (Isaiah 60: 1)*. The new life you have been given is another opportunity to arise and shine, and a privilege for you to live for the glory of God and be fulfilled in life,

> *"...for the gift of God is eternal life through Jesus Christ our Lord" (Romans 6: 23).*

How does Jesus Christ model the above statement in its truest form? The explanation dates back to the beginning of time at the inception of man. And this provides us with priceless insight into the process Satan used to sway man's dependence away from God by usurping the authority vested to man over the earth. Satan planted a seed of doubt about the meaning of God's instruction by saying,

> *"... Yea hath God said, ye shall not eat of every tree of the garden?" (Genesis 3: 1).*

By so saying, he attempted and influenced Eve capturing her mind away from God's clear statement of intent. If you noticed, you will discover he actually distorted God's statement by saying, *"...ye shall not eat of every tree of the garden."* This he did, so he could get the attention of Eve and gain a conversation with her. You must be careful of indulging in a conversation with a stranger and also bear in mind the consequences of your utterances. *In other words*, learn to bridle your tongue always and gauge your utterances before you speak. For there is a time to keep quiet not uttering a word, and also a time to speak. Cautiously know that when you do speak, you must make sure you are measuring and speaking the right words in the name of Jesus that will edify your hearers and bring glory to God.

The Bible says,

> *"Let the word of Christ dwell in you richly in all wisdom..." (Colossians 3: 16; see also 1 Thessalonians 2: 13).*

Although Satan's statement was very close to God's words; that was not what God had said to Adam. And Eve knew it but could not caution Satan even though she got firsthand information from Adam regarding the tree of the knowledge of good and evil. She was not there when God instructed Adam concerning the tree. Not even Adam who was knowledgeable and present at the scene could intervene to caution Satan and say this is what God said concerning what to eat and what not to eat in the garden:

> *"16And the LORD God commanded the man, saying, Of every tree of the garden thou mayest freely eat: 17But of the tree of the knowledge of good and evil, thou shalt not eat of it: for in the day that thou eatest thereof thou shalt surely die" (Genesis 2: 16-17).*

Adam could have intervened by shunning Satan and gotten him off his tuff knowing that the garden belonged to him, but he didn't. And so, Satan took advantage of the situation and directly contradicted God's statement knowing that a minute's shift of wordings was all he needed to convince Eve and convey a message that carried exactly the opposite in meaning, and by so doing implied that God was withholding something good and essential from them. Satan was invariably saying to them how could they depend on a God who withholds the truth from them because in Genesis 3: 6, the Bible lists three "goods" about the fruit:

(1) It was good for food
(2) It was pleasing to the eyes
(3) And it was desirable for gaining wisdom.

Satan knew there was nothing "wrong" with the fruit, but that it was the wrong way to a right destination knowing God had said to them not to eat of it. How can you reconcile that it was when Satan drew Eve's attention to the tree that she could see all the qualities of the tree that has always been there with them:

> *"And when the woman saw that the tree was good for food, and that it was pleasant to the eyes, and a tree to be desired to make one wise..."* (Genesis 3: 6).

The Bible is letting us into a revelation here; the woman had to see what she never took notice of before, of the tree that she had always played with. Her attention was enticed to the tree and at the point of seeing; she saw all the wrong things the enemy wanted her to see. These are qualities that seemingly looked good because her attention swayed was drawn to the tree in disguise. 1 John 2: 16-17 further clarifies this:

> *"16For all that is in the world, the lust of the flesh, and the lust of the eyes, and the pride of life, are not of the Father, but is of the world. 17And the world passeth away, and the lust thereof: but he that doeth the will of God abideth forever."*

Satan knew that Adam and Eve by disobeying their dependence on God would lose their covering and die. Remember Satan is a spirit and was once an angel of light like every angel in heaven designed to live forever. He was cast away from heaven and hauled to earth for his disobedience and that clothed him with darkness, and reserved him and his followers for the day of judgement on which they will burn perpetually in hell. So he knew the consequences of disobedience:

- Firstly, he knew that Adam and Eve would lose their *'life on earth forever living cherubic glory'* with which they were clothed because mankind was designed by God to live forever on earth like the angels in heaven. The earth was to be mankind's domain just as the heavenlies are for the angels. This 'life on earth forever living cherubic clothing' was the covering of the glory of God upon mankind that reveals the presence of God in man on earth meant for mankind's authority and perpetual existence. Which means that God did not make man in any way an inferior specie to suffer and die but the consequences of his disobedience brought sin and death into the world. Think for a minute beloved of God; *would God have made Adam an inferior specie in his own image and likeness?*

- *Why would God claim to love only to make mankind to live in sin; suffering saddled with sickness, infirmity, diseases and to die? Do you now see that something went wrong with man because of his indulgence; that he brought this judgment upon himself when he strayed from the presence of God in disobedience?* But, thanks to God, there is a remedy and hope for all mankind once again. This reassures that the miracle of life which is the gift of God is eternal life through Christ Jesus. This life in Christ when lived in obedience will protect the believer from every evil appearance, and eschew them from indulgences of sin and eternal death; making the believer to live the God kind of life on earth to the full.

- Secondly, because he Satan had been hauled to earth, clothed with darkness, and rejected of God. Adam and Eve's disobedience will simply mean them saying there are other ways to achieve much of what God has to offer. Which will now give him an advantage to disrupt Adam's position with God, by taking away their *'life on earth forever living cherubic glory'* and bringing destruction to the earth since Adam deliberately gave him the right. This disruption of Adam's position with God is the unclothing of the *'life on earth forever living cherubic glory of God known as eternal life'* that was once the grace upon mankind at creation with which he was to live forever. This was stripped off him in the garden when he willingly yielded to Eve's disobedience and submitted to Satan; causing the catastrophe that resulted in all mankind's death. Notably, it reveals exactly what Jesus' death represents. Jesus died so all mankind can be reinstated and live like God intended which is the essence of this gift of God that is life without an end in Christ Jesus our Lord. Obviously, the only way to have this eternal life and abide forever is to do the will of God and accept that God atoned for your sin on the cross in the person of our Lord Jesus Christ.
- Another remarkable point of note is that it was the Lord God who put the man in charge of the garden to tend and keep it. This indicates that the garden would have been man's forever if he had obeyed a simple instruction because God meant for him to keep it forever.

> *"¹⁵And the LORD God took the man, and put him into the Garden of Eden to dress it and to keep it"* (Genesis 2: 15).

Evidently, the tree of the knowledge of good and evil was the genesis of disobedience, sin and death. This is so because the tempter came to Eve and brought confusion that made her and her husband eat of the fruit of the tree against God's instructions. And for this reasons they lost their position with God, their authority over all created things and the right of perpetual abode on earth. *How did we come to this conclusion?* The Bible gives us an insight thus:

> "*19 And out of the ground the LORD God formed every beast of the field, and every fowl of the air; and brought them unto Adam to see what he would call them: and whatsoever Adam called every living creature, that was the name thereof. 20 And Adam gave names to all cattle and to the fowl of the air, and to every beast of the field...*" (Genesis 2: 19-20).

There is no gainsaying that Adam was bestowed with the highest authority and responsibility befitting to man. He gaining the approval of Almighty God was learning to be like God by exercising his faith which enabled him to name all the created works of God through godly wisdom and revelation knowledge.

> *26 And God said, Let us make man in our image, after our likeness: and let them have dominion over the fish of the sea, and over the fowl of the air, and over the cattle, and over all the earth, and over every creeping thing that creepeth upon the earth. 27 So God created man in his own image, in the image of God created he him; male and female created he them. 28 And God blessed them, and God said unto them, Be fruitful, and multiply, and replenish the earth, and subdue it: and have dominion over the fish of the sea, and over the fowl of the air, and over every living thing that moveth upon the earth (Genesis 1: 26-28).*

CHUCKS UZONWANNE

Invariably, God clothed man with his *'life on earth forever living cherubic glory'* and positioned him to have dominion and subdue the earth. Which means man was clothed with divine presence and had the authority to speak to the created order and they will obey. Since man was made to live forever, he wouldn't have had need to lack, be sick and die. But because man refused to obey the creator, the earth and all creation revolted against Adam's authority over them.

Listen to their conversation and learn never to underestimate the power of the one who wants you to depend on anything but God.

> *¹Now the serpent was more subtle than any beast of the field which the LORD God had made. And he said unto the woman, Yea, hath God said, ye shall not eat of every tree of the garden? ²And the woman said unto the serpent, We may eat of the fruit of the trees of the garden: ³But of the fruit of the tree which is in the midst of the garden, God hath said, Ye shall not eat of it, neither shall ye touch it, lest ye die. ⁴And the serpent said unto the woman, Ye shall not surely die: ⁵For God doth know that in the day ye eat thereof, then your eyes shall be opened, and ye shall be as gods, knowing good and evil. ⁶And when the woman saw that the tree was good for food, and that it was pleasant to the eyes, and a tree to be desired to make one wise, she took of the fruit thereof, and did eat, and gave also unto her husband with her; and he did eat. ⁷And the eyes of them both were opened, and they knew that they were naked; and they sewed fig leaves together, and made themselves aprons (Genesis 3: 1-7).*

The Bible explains why the tree is called the tree of the knowledge of good and evil because it grants you revelation knowledge to decipher between good and evil. The down side to the situation in the garden was that the devil used it as a ploy to:

- Deceive Adam and Eve by estranging them from their relationship with God.
- He stripped them of their clothed glory by lulling them into disobeying God.
- Because they were meant to represent right standing and godliness on earth. He made them lose their authority to enforce the system of righteousness over the earth.
- And finally, he usurped their birth right to represent and enforce righteousness; and so he became the god of this world system deceiving those that are without Christ Jesus.

> "*3But if our gospel be hid, it is hid to them that are lost: 4In whom the god of this world hath blinded the minds of them which believe not, lest the light of the glorious gospel of Christ, who is the image of God, should shine unto them*" (2 Corinthians 4: 3-4).

The question Eve ought to have asked herself was; *where did the tempter come from after all these years they've been in the garden with the Lord? And how come it is the very tree that God instructed them not to eat that the tempter pointed to them?* This would have helped her to reason before indulging in a conversation with a complete stranger. More so, indulging in a conversation she did not have accurate knowledge of. Does this sound familiar to you, and have you been there where you were instructed not to do a thing for certain reasons and you ended up doing it. *How did it make you feel? Where you remorseful, or proudly blaming someone else for your wrong deeds?* Look at it, the Bible said that suddenly Eve's desire longed for the fruit when she saw that the tree was good for food, pleasant to the eyes and able to make one wise, as a result, she ate of it and gave some to her husband. Damning the consequences of their action; they both indulged in disobedience and brought sin whose fruit is death on themselves and all mankind.

"For the wages of sin is death..." (Romans 6: 23).

Always bear in mind one of the key importance for which Eve fitted into the picture of existence was so she and Adam could procreate, and through them the whole earth would be populated. Since they have fallen to sin, this will have a rub-off on all generations unless God did something to revoke the generational sin whose wages is death. And so in trying to resolve the issue, God said:

"And I will put enmity between thee and the woman,
and between thy seed and her seed; it shall bruise thy head,
and thou shalt bruise his heel" (Genesis 3: 15).

When God made the above statement, he foresaw himself coming into the world as the seed of the woman who would come in the flesh to bruise the head of the Devil since the contention was between the Devil, Adam and the estate God gave to Adam which is the earth.

How would God do this? Apparently, since there was no one else who could dispossess the Devil of what he stole from Adam, God volunteered himself in the person of his Son knowing he is an authority over the Devil. God knows that since Adam had bowed to the Devil and given him his rightful place; the Devil now has authority over Adam, his seed, and the right to the earth. The Bible says:

"Know ye not, that to whom ye yield yourselves servants
to obey, his servants ye are to whom ye obey..." (Romans 6:
16 see also Matthew 4: 1-11; Luke 4: 1-13).

And since there was not a higher authority over the Devil, because Adam the authorised owner of the earth had fallen, God now appointed a time when he would come to earth and redeem mankind. Reason being that it would have been improper and unsuitable for God to impose himself on the situation just like that or use anything less [lower] than man for man's restoration. This is because:

I.   *God is Spirit and would need to operate on man's level. And the only way for him to do so was to cloth himself with the nature of man.*
II. *He is God of order who does not break rank therefore will not break his word; he needs permission to act on man's behalf since man lost his bequeathed authority to an enemy.*
III. *He couldn't use an angel; he knows an angel was not qualified to rival the Devil because an angel was made lower than man and the Devil was once an Arch angel before his fall.*

One would wonder if an angel was indeed lower than man considering the scripture in Psalm 8: 4 - 5 that says: "What is man that thou art mindful of him? And the son of man that thou visitest him? For thou hast made him a little lower than the angels, and has crowned him with glory and honour" (See also Hebrews 2: 5 - 11). If you will quietly consider the questions in the scripture, and ponder on them for a while. Ask yourself, "who visited man? And how did God make man a little lower than the angels? Are you getting the revelation that explains how? This inference show that "a little lower" represents or means the earth. The Bible is merely giving an insight on how God made man to dominate the earth. And because the earth before God is a little lower than heaven, God crowned man with His glory and honour to have the highest authority over all created order (See also 1 Corinthians 6: 3). This is the reason why he made man in his image and likeness. Now ask yourself; if God made man in his image and likeness to be exactly like him; could he have made man lower than an angel? This is because an angel is a ministering spirit [servant to God and to man], and therefore cannot be superior to the sons of God (Hebrews 1: 4, 6 - 7. 13 - 14). This question can also be answered by the scripture in Psalm 82: 6 that says: "I have said, ye are gods; and all of you are children of the Most High [God]." I need you to relate and correlate the explanation of the scripture in Psalm 8: 4 - 5 to the insight we have been giving of Psalm 82: 6 and conclude by yourself (Psalm 91: 11; Matthew 13: 39 and 49; 18: 10; and Luke 20: 36). You will indeed agree that because man is a god after the semblance of Almighty Jehovah makes it absolutely impossible for an angel who is man's servant to be superior to man. A servant cannot be superior to his master (Matthew 10: 24; John 13: 16 and 15: 20). It is as a result of the value God placed in man that makes it impossible for an angel to be superior to man, which is why God shed his perfect blood so as to restore man back to his rightful position of authority over all created order.

Taking all enumerated factors into consideration, it becomes imperative to note that since the whole earth had been corrupted with sin and was dying, God knew that the only way to regain the authority was for him to die in the stead of all mankind. Knowing he has the power to lay down his life and the power to take it up again. Jesus affirms:

> "*17 Therefore doth my Father love me, because I lay down my life, that I might take it again. 18 No man taketh it from me, but I lay it down of myself. I have power to lay it down, and I have power to take it again. This commandment have I received of my Father*" (John 10: 17-18).

And so God came to earth in the person of Jesus at the fullness of time and died for the salvation and restoration of all mankind.

³Know ye not; that so many of us as were baptized into Jesus Christ were baptized into his death? ⁴Therefore we are buried with him by baptism into death: that like as Christ was raised up from the dead by the glory of the Father, even so we also should walk in newness of life. ⁵For if we have been planted together in the likeness of his death, we shall be also in the likeness of his resurrection: ⁶Knowing this, that our old man is crucified with him, that the body of sin might be destroyed, that henceforth we should not serve sin. ⁷For he that is dead is freed from sin. ⁸Now if we be dead with Christ, we believe that we shall also live with him: ⁹Knowing that Christ being raised from the dead dieth no more; death hath no more dominion over him. ¹⁰For in that he died, he died unto sin once but in that he liveth he liveth unto God forever (Romans 6: 3-10).

Evidently, God now has the right and authority over the earth field because he purchased it with his precious sinless blood. He paid the debt of sin owed by humanity with his life. This he accomplished on the cross of Calvary in the name of Jesus Christ. *Why in the name of Jesus?* You need to understand that Jesus is one of the Triune being right from the beginning of creation. He is the spoken word of God:

"For there are three that bear record in heaven, the Father, the Word, and the Holy Ghost: and these three are one" (1 John 5: 7).

And since God is Spirit and was coming to earth as a human being, he would need to be identified with a name. *Or have you ever seen anyone born into this world that is without a name?* This is the reason the Prophets of old herald his coming and foretold his name, and at the fullness of time when angel Gabriel appeared to Mary he confirmed his name. And so the name 'Jesus' was given to the manifested word of God to tell him apart and identify him as the Saviour with the anointing who would take away the sins of all mankind.

> *[17]For God sent not his Son [word] into the world to condemn the world; but that the world through him might be saved. [18]He that believeth on him is not condemned but he that believeth not is condemned already, because he hath not believed in the name of the only begotten Son of God (John 3: 17-18).*

Before the advent of Jesus no human being bore the name 'Jesus' until after his death, burial and resurrection. His death on the cross was God's perfect plan to defeat the devil. No one before the coming of Jesus came to save mankind only Jesus came to seek and to save that which was lost. Our Lord Jesus himself affirmed this by saying,

> *"For the Son of man is come to seek and to save that which was lost." (Luke 19: 10).*

Evidently, Jesus is the living word of God, the redeemer of all mankind. This means anyone who believes in Jesus and confesses him as Lord and Saviour is clothed with redemption, glory and authority over all the works of the Devil. Sickness, infirmity, diseases, and even eternal death are alienated in his life. He has conquered death and has the right to reign in life both here on earth and in eternity with God. Remember that God is Spirit and if he is to represent man he must stripe himself of his glory and experience the fallen state of man. This explains two things:

1. *This is the essence for his being tempted by Satan (Luke 4: 1-13; see also Matthew 4: 1-11).*

2. *This also means that when Jesus hung on the cross, he hung on the cross as a Man and not as God which was why he could cry out:*

   "...Eli, Eli, lama sabachthani? That is to say, My God, my God, why hast thou forsaken me?" (Matthew 27: 46).

The significance of this is when Jesus hung on the cross; the sin of the whole world was laid upon him. Sin is spiritual, so it couldn't have been on his physical body but upon his Spirit. And because God is holy and would not behold sin; he turned his face away from Jesus and forsook him so the scriptures might be fulfilled.

   "He, who knew no sin, was made sin for us..." (2 Corinthians 5: 21).

You need to realise that at this point when he died on the cross he did not die as God but as a man. It would have been impossible for him to have died as God because God is Spirit and cannot die. A spirit cannot die, and that accounts for when Jesus died on the cross as a man; he went to hell on our behalf and there he discomfited the Devil.

The Lord Jesus Christ regained Adam's lost glory and authority when he rose triumphantly from the dead. He restored and has bestowed it to all who believe in him. This is what the miracle of life is all about. This indicates that no one who believes in Jesus will die and go to hell.

Why did Jesus go to hell? He went to hell on behalf of everyone who believes in him so they don't have to go to hell. And he conquered death, so they don't have to die eternally. It is only those who don't believe in Jesus that will go to hell and taste the second death themselves.

²¹Then said Martha unto Jesus, Lord, if thou hadst been here, my brother had not died. ²²But I know, that even now, whatsoever thou wilt ask of God, God will give it thee. ²³Jesus saith unto her, Thy brother shall rise again. ²⁴Martha saith unto him, I know that he shall rise again in the resurrection at the last day. ²⁵Jesus said unto her, I AM THE RESURRECTION, AND THE LIFE: HE THAT BELIEVETH IN ME, THOUGH HE WERE DEAD, YET SHALL HE LIVE: ²⁶AND WHOSOEVER LIVETH AND BELIEVETH IN ME SHALL NEVER DIE (John 11: 21-26).

This insightfully reveals that anyone who is in Christ will not go to hell or die the second death.

"²⁰But now is Christ risen from the dead, and become the first fruits of them that slept. ²¹For since by man came death, by man came also the resurrection of the dead. ²²For as in Adam all die, even so in Christ shall all be made alive" (1 Corinthians 15: 20-22).

"⁸But God commendeth his love toward us, in that, while we were yet sinners, Christ died for us. ⁹Much more then, being now justified by his blood, we shall be saved from wrath through him. ¹⁰For if, when we were enemies, we were reconciled to God by the death of his Son, much more, being reconciled, we shall be saved by his life.

¹¹And not only so, but we also joy in God through our Lord Jesus Christ, by whom we have now received the atonement. ¹²Wherefore, as by one man sin entered into the world, and death by sin; and so death passed upon all men, for that all have sinned: ¹³(For until the law sin *was in the world: but sin is not imputed when there is no law. ¹⁴Nevertheless death reigned from Adam to Moses, even over them that had not sinned after the similitude of Adam's transgression, who is the figure of him that was to come. ¹⁵But not as the offence, so also is the free gift. For if through the offence of one many be dead, much more the grace of God, and the gift by grace, which is by one man, Jesus Christ, hath abounded unto many. ¹⁶And not as it was by one that sinned, so is the gift: for the judgment was by one to condemnation, but the free gift is of many offences unto justification. ¹⁷For if by one man's offence death reigned by one; much more they which receive abundance of grace and of the gift of righteousness shall reign in life by one, Jesus Christ. ¹⁸Therefore as by the offence of one judgment came upon all men to condemnation; even so by the righteousness of one the free gift came upon all men unto justification of life. ¹⁹For as by one man's disobedience many were made sinners, so by the obedience of one shall many be made righteous" (Romans 5: 8-19).*

By this I emphasised that if you have received Jesus Christ as your Lord and Saviour, you will not go to hell because Jesus went on your behalf. This is because you are now living his life:

> *"¹⁴...And God hath both raised up the Lord, and will also raise up us by his own power... ¹⁷But he that is joined unto the Lord is one spirit... ¹⁹What? know ye not that your body is the temple of the Holy Ghost which is in you, which ye have of God, and ye are not your own?²⁰For ye are bought with a price: therefore glorify God in your body, and in your spirit, which are God's" (1 Corinthians 6: 14-20).*

"*⁴Therefore we are buried with him by baptism into death: that like as Christ was raised up from the dead by the glory of the Father, even so we also should walk in newness of life. ⁵For if we have been planted together in the likeness of his death, we shall be also in the likeness of his resurrection: ⁶Knowing this, that our old man is crucified with him, that the body of sin might be destroyed, that henceforth we should not serve sin. ⁷For he that is dead is freed from sin. ⁸Now if we be dead with Christ, we believe that we shall also live with him: ⁹Knowing that Christ being raised from the dead dieth no more; death hath no more dominion over him. ¹⁰For in that he died, he died unto sin once: but in that he liveth, he liveth unto God. ¹¹Likewise reckon ye also yourselves to be dead indeed unto sin, but alive unto God through Jesus Christ our Lord*" (Romans 6: 4-11; see also 1 Thessalonians 4: 14, 5: 9-10; 2 Timothy 2: 11; 1 Peter 3: 18).

CHAPTER FIVE

THE MANIFESTATION OF GOD'S WORD

*H*ow did God manifest his word? Evidently, God is Spirit, for him to manifest his word means he would have to come to earth in a human body since that was his intent when he spoke in the garden. This he did knowing it was the only way he could come to redeem man and dispossess the Devil of Adam's right and stop generational death in hell. And the Bible tells us how he manifested his word in a human body:

> "*30And the angel said unto her, Fear not, Mary for thou hast found favour with God. 31And, behold, thou shalt conceive in thy womb, and bring forth a son, and shalt call his name JESUS. 32He shall be great, and shall be called the Son of the Highest: and the Lord God shall give unto him the throne of his father David: 33And he shall reign over the house of Jacob for ever; and of his kingdom there shall be no end*" (Luke 1: 30-33).

This is consequent upon the fact that when Adam and Eve sinned they lost their life on earth forever cherubic glory; and everything in nature partook of their sin, putting on darkness, sin and death. This also conjoins there was nothing that could appease God and atone for their sin other than an uncontaminated blood which only God has. So when God shed the blood of an animal in the garden, it was symbolic of what he did on the cross to clothe mankind and to wash them from their sin since they lost their glory to the Devil. This is why the blood of Jesus is the perfect sacrifice and the only blood that cleanses and makes whole. It remits and atones for the sins of all who believe and receive him into their hearts.

"Unto him that loved us and has washed us from our sins in his own blood" (Revelation 1: 5).

"...for it is the blood that maketh an atonement for the soul" (Leviticus 17: 11). "...for without the shedding of blood there is no remission of sin" (Hebrews 9: 23).

At the fullness of time when the Angel came to Mary saying, *"³⁰... Fear not, Mary: for thou hast found favour with God. ³¹And, behold, thou shalt conceive in thy womb, and bring forth a son, and shalt call his name JESUS... ³⁴Then said Mary unto the angel, How shall this be, seeing I know not a man? ³⁵And the angel answered and said unto her, The Holy Ghost shall come upon thee, and the power of the Highest shall overshadow thee: therefore also that holy thing which shall be born of thee shall be called the Son of God" (Luke 1: 30-35).*

Going by the scriptures, it is evidently clear that a virgin by name Mary found favour with God and became the vessel of grace through whom he brought his word to manifestation. *How did God do it?* Mary was overshadowed by the Most High God through the agency of his Holy Spirit and she conceived by the power of his spoken word and gave birth to a prophetically long awaited Son named Jesus Christ according to the predictions of the Angel.

"[18]Now the birth of Jesus Christ was on this wise: when as his mother Mary was espoused to Joseph, before they came together [had intercourse], she was found with child of the Holy Ghost...[20]But while Joseph thought on these things, behold, the angel of the Lord appeared unto him in a dream, saying, Joseph, thou son of David, fear not to take unto thee Mary thy wife: for that which is conceived in her is of the Holy Ghost.

[21]And she shall bring forth a son and thou shall call his name Jesus: for he shall save his people from their sins. [22]Now all this was done, that it might be fulfilled which was spoken of the Lord by the prophet Isaiah (see Isaiah 7: 14, 9: 6-7), [23]saying, Behold, a virgin shall conceive, and bear a son, and shall call his name Emmanuel, which being interpreted is, God with us" (Matthew 1: 18, 20-23).

With these scriptures, we deduce that Jesus came for one purpose and one purpose only; to die for the sins of all mankind and save for eternity all those who would confess him as their Lord and saviour. Knowing that God has redeemed us from the curse of the land, we became the sons of God the moment we received him into our hearts, for the Bible says:

"But as many as received him, to them gave he power to become the sons of God, even to them that believe in his name" (John 1: 12)

"[8]But what saith it? The word is nigh thee, even in thy mouth, and thy heart: that is, the word of faith, which we preach (see also Deut. 30: 14); [9]That if thou shall confess with thy mouth the Lord Jesus, and shall believe in

CHUCKS UZONWANNE

thine heart that God hath raised him from the dead, thou shall be saved. [10]For with the heart man believeth unto righteousness; and with the mouth confession is made unto salvation" (Romans 10: 8 - 10)

This scripture is saying, if we will trust in the word of God and confess the Lordship of Jesus over our sinful nature, that is, if we will be honest and acknowledge we are sinners (see Romans 3: 23), God is faithful and just to forgive us our sins, and to cleanse us from all unrighteousness. This is because anybody born of God does not commit sin for God's word Jesus who is the finished work of redemption dwells in him (see also 1 John 3: 9). This is his intent for coming, to save all mankind and to fulfil the scriptures. The Bible says:

"[6]Knowing this, that our old man is crucified with him, that the body of sin might be destroyed, that henceforth we should not serve sin [7]For he that is dead is freed from sin. [8]Now if we be dead with Christ, we believe that we shall also live with him: [9]Knowing that Christ being raised from the dead dieth no more; death hath no more dominion over him. [10]For in that he died, he died unto sin once but in that he liveth he liveth unto God. [11]Likewise reckon ye also yourselves to be dead indeed unto sin, but alive unto God through Jesus Christ our Lord. [12]Let not sin therefore reign in your mortal body, that ye should obey it in the lusts thereof. [13]Neither yield ye your members as instruments of unrighteousness unto sin but yield yourselves unto God as those that are alive from the dead and your members as instruments of righteousness unto God. [14]For sin shall not have dominion over you; for ye are not under the law, but under grace" (Romans 6: 6-14).

Jesus who knew no sin was made sin for all mankind; he became the perfect sacrificial Lamb of God who took away the sins of the whole world once and for all. There are three reasons Jesus is the atoned perfect sacrifice for all mankind:

I. *God did say that the seed of the woman will bruise the head of Satan, even as Satan will bruise his heel (Genesis 3: 15). Jesus is that seed! When he hung on the cross, he was pierced on his side with a spear, and water and blood was released signifying the washing of our sins and the pleading for our restoration. He died and went to hell for the sakes of all mankind and there stripped the Devil of our rights and resurrected triumphantly on the third day. This also reveals that whilst Jesus was engaged in battle in hell with the Devil, he was at the same time bridging the gap between God and man by asking God to see all mankind with the eyes of grace through his shed blood.*

II. *Without the shedding of blood, there is no remission of sin (Hebrews 9: 23). Jesus became sin for us and shed his precious blood for the redemption of all (2 Corinthians 5: 21). With his blood we were washed from our sins and are now covered with the glory of God (Revelation 1: 5). We have been restored with grace to live the newness of life (Romans 8: 1-2). This newness of life is the life of God that never dies found only in Christ Jesus. Anyone who is in Christ will not die and go to hell because Jesus already went to hell and conquered hell on our behalf thereby giving us eternal life (John 14: 6 & 1 Peter 1: 23).*

III. *The only perfect sacrifice would have to be a sinless blood without contamination which Jesus had and the Bible reckons saying, "...Unto him that loved us, and washed us from our sins in his own blood..." (Revelation 1: 5; see also 2 Corinthians 5: 21).*

CHUCKS UZONWANNE

This is exactly what the Bible mean when it says:

¹For the law having a shadow of good things to come, and not the very image of the things, can never with those sacrifices which they offered year by year continually make the comers thereunto perfect. ²For then would they not have ceased to be offered? Because that the worshippers once purged should have had no more conscience of sins. ³But in those sacrifices there is a remembrance again made of sins every year. ⁴For it is not possible that the blood of bulls and of goats should take away sins. ⁵Wherefore when he cometh into the world, he saith, sacrifice and offering thou wouldest not, but a body hast thou prepared me: ⁶In burnt offerings and sacrifices for sin thou hast had no pleasure. ⁷Then said I, Lo, I come (in the volume of the book it is written of me,) to do thy will, O God. ⁸Above when he said, Sacrifice and offering and burnt offerings and offering for sin thou wouldest not, neither hadst pleasure therein; which are offered by the law; ⁹Then said he, Lo, I come to do thy will, O God. He taketh away the first that he may establish the second. ¹⁰By which will, we are sanctified through the offering of the body of Jesus Christ once for all. ¹¹And every priest standeth daily ministering and offering oftentimes the same sacrifices, which can never take away sins: ¹²But this man [Jesus], after he had offered one sacrifice for sins forever, sat down on the right hand of God (Hebrew 10: 1-12) (See also Psalm 40: 5-8).

One would have wondered if there was no other means God would have employed to bring redemption to mankind. God would have happily used an angel if it were possible for an angel to atone for man's sins and carry-out the perfect sacrifice, but because an angel is a ministering spirit [a servant] and lower than man, it therefore became imperative that an angel was not qualified.

Neither was it possible for the blood of bulls and calves to atone for the sins of mankind because bulls and calves were also affected by the sin caused by Adam and Eve and therefore had blemishes and were also subjected to the laws of sin and death. This is responsible for the continual offering of burnt offerings and sacrifices for sin that did not make any difference because it was repeated year in year out without significance. But when our Lord Jesus stepped into the Holy of holies with his own uncontaminated sinless blood, he perfected once and for all the sacrifice for all mankind. All sins were abolished in Christ Jesus; therefore, never will there be any need for sacrifices of blood on God's altar of righteousness other than the sacrifices of our lip. (See also Galatians 1: 4; Hebrews 7: 27; 1: 3-4, 2: 27; Matthew 1: 21, 9: 6). This means man was made exclusively to represent God on earth with authority over all created order until man lost his bearing and the enemy usurped his position. You need to bear in mind, there are those who are watching and waiting for you to lose your place so they can occupy; so *be sober and vigilant for your adversary the Devil is walking about seeking whom he may devour (1 Peter 5: 8).*

With this in mind, prayer must be the inevitable and paramount thing in the life of every believer. Prayer is the utmost power to overcome the enemy, so be prayerful. Also know that the only thing that can wash away the sins of mankind is an uncontaminated blood that God alone has, because when man sinned everything in creation partook of sin and rebelled against the order of creation, and God was left with the resolve to give his own blood which is why the Bible says in Revelation 1:5,

> *"...Unto Him that loved us, and washed us from our sins in his own blood"* (See also Galatians 1: 4; 1 Peter 2: 24; 1 John 2: 2).

CHUCKS UZONWANNE

For God to have given his own blood, he had to assume man's falling state and this enabled him fulfil his own word. *Why?* We must always remember that God is Spirit and to experience man's falling state without sinning he must put on the form of a man to operate on man's level:

> *"For we have not an high priest which cannot be touched with the feeling of our infirmities; but was in all points tempted like as we are, yet without sin" (Hebrews 4: 15) (see also 1 John 3: 5; 1 Peter 3: 18).*

This implies that when he came to earth, he became our sin and shed his own blood as the perfect sacrifice for the atonement of the sins of all mankind by dying on the cross. The Bible says:

> *"And ye know that he was manifested to take away our sins; and in him is no sin" (1 John 3: 5).*

> *"For He had made him to be seen for us, who knew no sin; that we might be made the righteousness of God in Him"* (2 Corinthians 5: 21).

> *"Who did no sin, neither was guile found in his mouth: Who, when he was reviled, reviled not again; when he suffered, he threatened not; but committed himself to him that judgeth righteously: Who his own self bare our sins in his own body on the tree, that we, being dead to sins, should live unto righteousness: by whose stripes ye were healed" (1Peter 2: 22 – 24).*

If you correlate the desire of God to restore man; you will understand more of this wonderful story of what brought about the birth of Jesus. Now, we are all aware that God is his word and his word cannot return to him void (See Isaiah 55: 10-11). So, he appointed a time to bring his word Jesus Christ as remedy for our sins to fruition taking cognisance of what he said in Genesis 3: 15. He accomplished that through the annunciation of Jesus, which is why the Bible declared saying,

> *"...For this purpose the son of God was manifested [appeared], that he might destroy the works of the devil"* (1 John 3: 8).

This glorious atonement opened the door of our destiny and restored our relationship with God, giving us authority over the works of the enemy. With it, we are ushered into God's holy of holies through the shed blood of Jesus Christ on Calvary's cross and that sealed us with the love of God which we received by grace and right standing as a result of our believing in Jesus Christ and confessing him as our Lord and Saviour. When the Bible declared *"the battle is of the Lord"*, this is what he was referring to; that mankind was going to be re-instated and given authority to have rulership on earth as God originally intended it. Just like in the Garden of Eden, the enemy might try to resist thinking that when Jesus hung on the cross that it was over with redemption, but God raised a standard enabling Jesus to go to hell and discomfit Satan and on the third day resurrected triumphantly. This is what it's all about, the miracle of life is for all, but not all will see eternal life. Eternal life is only for those who believe that:

> *"God sent his Son into the world not to condemn the world, but that the world through him might be saved. He that believeth on him is not condemned: but he that believeth not is condemned already, because he hath not believed in the name of the only begotten Son of God."* (John 3: 17 - 18).

This means unless you are born again, you will not see nor enter into the kingdom of God.

> *³Jesus answered and said unto him, Verily, verily, I say unto thee, except a man be born again, he cannot see the kingdom of God. ⁴Nicodemus saith unto him, how can a man be born when he is old? Can he enter the second time into his mother's womb, and be born? ⁵Jesus answered, Verily, verily, I say unto thee, except a man be born of water and of the [Holy] Spirit, he cannot enter into the kingdom of God (John 3: 3-5).*

CHAPTER SIX

MAN IN THE CIRCLE OF LIFE

T he secret of life is with the Almighty Creator, the maker of all things. He is the Father of all spirits and the owner of the breath in every human person. There is something about life that's mysterious which ordinarily cannot be explained from the periphery, yet cannot be overlooked. This is because some people see life as a reality that has to be lived reverently in righteousness and holiness through prayer to maintain an intimacy with Almighty Creator. While some others see God as a myth and claim he does not exist. These others see life as non-existent because of the figment of their misconstrued imagination due to their evil darkened minds, and so they treat life with levity and sinfully. This perhaps for some reason explains the motive behind the basis these others are incessantly busy trying to disprove the existence of Almighty Creator by reasoning out creation with their senses, which further explains why they go to the moon and other planets, and in laboratories looking for something they could use as evidence to disprove God's existence. The truth is that they are deluded and because of their delusion; every way they turn they're greeted with illusion, disappointment and awesome mysteries that arrest their presumptions.

Interestingly, I got talking with a medical doctor who happens to be the head of a fertility and surgical section in a major hospital in London who in his own words said to me, 'it is an honour to meet a minister of the gospel, someone who believes and talks about God,' as a matter of fact, 'this is my first time of meeting with a pastor in all my life as a medical doctor.' He said and went further to say that over 200 years ago since the innovation of medicine till date, medical science and medical doctors are still in awe at the mystery behind man in the circle of life. He said only God is the creator of life because medicine have tried to disprove the existence of God and to play his role but cannot because of human limitations. He then sited an instance of how the egg in the ovary of a woman can only be helped to replicate and produce as long as there is an active egg still remaining or found in the ovary. He said, 'once there are no more eggs, medical science is handicapped and cannot produce eggs [life] by itself.' He went further to emphasise that 'there's no medicine or science able to produce life in whatever form, itself.' Then he said something very remarkable and amusing, 'he would have become 'God' if that were possible'.

Excitedly, he interestingly said, 'this is what every medical doctor tries to be but cannot because of the amazing complexity of the mystery in the circle of life.' When he said that, the Holy Spirit ministered to me saying, 'God is the Chief Surgeon and the only architect of life and medical science knows it.' The Holy Spirit then referred me to Genesis and Ezekiel:

> "*21And the LORD God caused a deep sleep to fall upon Adam and he slept: and he took one of his ribs, and closed up the flesh instead thereof; 22And the rib, which the LORD God had taken from man, made he a woman...*"(Genesis 2: 21-22; see also Ezekiel 37: 1-14; Mathew 4: 23; Mark 10: 46-52 see also John 9: 1-11).

"⁵Thus saith the Lord GOD unto these bones; Behold, I will cause breath to enter into you, and ye shall live: ⁶And I will lay sinews upon you, and will bring up flesh upon you, and cover you with skin, and put breath in you, and ye shall live; and ye shall know that I am the LORD (Ezekiel 37: 5-6).

As the Holy Spirit took me through scriptures, giving me instances of God's surgical services to man, it became evidently apparent that God was the first surgeon ever to sedate and operate on a human being. He could even put flesh and sinews on dead bones and make them come alive.

Proving positive that medical science is merely learning the things that God had already done and put in place. My acquainted medical doctor; a jolly fellow kept me the more enlightened about medical discoveries and the need for man to revere God. He talked so much about the wonders of God and how medical science tries to understand new discoveries both in science and in human beings in relation to the existence of God that I was moved to ask him if he believed in God. In response, he beamed with a smile and then said, 'yes, I do; I believe in God.' And he further said, 'Anyone who does not believe in God and his existence, science or medicine is merely deluding themselves.' As a minister of the gospel, I of course concur, since I know quite a number of practising medical doctors who are avowed believers in Christ Jesus.

Now, I need you to humble yourself and hear what God says:

¹...the heaven is my throne, and the earth is my footstool...²For all those things hath mine hand made... saith the LORD" (Isaiah 66: 1-2).

CHUCKS UZONWANNE

"⁴Then the word of the LORD came unto me, saying, ⁵Before I formed thee in the belly I knew thee; and before thou camest forth out of the womb I sanctified thee" (Jeremiah 1: 4-5).

These previews are revelatory, and make it abundantly clear that God exists and he is the source of all life because no medical science has been able to accomplish these fits. And evidently proves that the seal of the authorship of life is with the Almighty God, creator and maker of all things. This apparently goes further to show that Jehovah the Supreme Ruler of the earth owns the entire Milky Way, planets and galaxies and is the Father of all Spirits. This is the truth! God is the Source of all life who made man in his image and likeness and is in control of the breath in every human being. The Psalmist lends credence to this,

"Know ye that the LORD he is God: it is he that hath made us, and not we ourselves; we are his people and the sheep of his pasture" (Psalm 100: 3).

Making it abundantly clear for those who are seeking means to disprove the existence of God to be more confounded. This is because they do not know God can only be found by those who seek him in truth and in spirit. And can only be accomplished through the miracle of knowing Jesus. And our Lord Jesus confirming this declares:

"⁶... I am the way, the truth, and the life: no man cometh unto the Father, but by me. ⁷If ye had known me, ye should have known my Father also: ... ⁹He that hath seen me hath seen the Father...¹⁰The words that I speak unto you I speak not of myself: but the Father that dwelleth in me, he doeth the works. ¹¹Believe me that I am in the

Father, and the Father in me: or else believe me for the
very works' sake" (John 14: 6-11).

These scriptures are as elaborate as they can get, but for the sakes of those who are yet to get it, a further illustration is required. Here the Lord Jesus stamps the seal of our relationship with the Father to be found only in him *'I am the way, the truth, and the life: no man cometh unto the Father but by me...'* Indeed, no man can come to the Father except by Jesus. He went further to say, *'He that hath seen me hath seen the Father,'* implying that he and the Father are one and the same. In crowning his statement, Jesus took it one step further when he said,

> *"...the words that I speak unto you I speak not of myself: but the Father that dwelleth in me, he doeth the works" (John 14: 10).*

This invariably means when you listen to the words of Jesus, you are listening to the words spoken by God the Father himself. This grants us a revelation to know that whenever Jesus speaks it is the same as when the Father is speaking because both of them are one *"I and my Father are one" (John 10: 30). '...Believe me that I am in the Father and the Father in me...' (John 14: 11).*

When you get to heaven you will not see Jesus apart from the Father. This is because he is integral with the Father. Jesus is the spoken word of God the Father and the name 'Jesus' is only recognized here on earth for identity purposes. This name existed to save all that will believe and call upon him in spirit and in truth for their salvation because of the barrier which sin placed against all mankind. This can be further explained in the scripture that says,

> *"Neither is there salvation in any other: for there is none other name under heaven given among men, whereby*

we must be saved" (Acts 4: 12; see also Acts 10: 43 and Matthew 1: 21).

It is only through the name of Jesus that salvation can be given to men for them to be saved. *Hear what Apostle Paul* says:

> *³For this is good and acceptable in the sight of God our Saviour; ⁴Who will have all men to be saved, and to come unto the knowledge of the truth. ⁵For there is one God and one mediator between God and men, the man Christ Jesus ⁶Who gave himself a ransom for all, to be testified in due time (1 Timothy 2: 3-6).*

Have you ever sat down to think how wonderfully you are made and what is it that makes you who you are? The Bible affirms that you are fearfully and wonderfully made:

> *¹³For thou hast possessed my reins: thou hast covered me in my mother's womb. ¹⁴I will praise thee; for I am fearfully and wonderfully made: marvellous are thy works; and that my soul knoweth right well. ¹⁵My substance was not hid from thee, when I was made in secret, and curiously wrought in the lowest parts of the earth. ¹⁶Thine eyes did see my substance, yet being imperfect [unperfected]; and in thy book all my members were written, which in continuance were fashioned, when as yet there was none of them. ¹⁷How precious also are thy thoughts unto me, O God! How great is the sum of them! (Psalm 139: 13-17).*

If you will digest this thought, it will bring out the very best of you and boost your paradigm to see God with the annals of his love. This will also reveal your uniqueness in ways that you begin to see life on earth as a gift from God and a journey for intimacy as it defines the process of our growing in God, being completely made whole in him.

As you ponder on God's creation, the beauty of life and its intent, you will begin to discover that this unmerited grace opened the door of human destiny to be significant, successful and great by the dictates and perfect will of God. You will also begin to understand what the miracle of life is all about; of how man came to be in the circle of life.

The miracle of life is about you! The existence of man in the circle of life is about the love of God for humanity, and how God personified himself in a human body

> *"And God said; Let us make man in our image, after our likeness: and let them have dominion..."* (Genesis 1: 26).

This is why angels in heaven applaud and rejoice at the miracle of the new birth called 'everlasting life' whenever a sinner repents and receive salvation because it is the God kind of life in a human person. Mind you, it was God who chose to make man in his reflection after his resemblance to represent him on earth which was the reason man was giving dominion to have rulership on earth just as God has dominion over all creation both in heaven and on earth.

CHAPTER SEVEN

THE NEW BIRTH MIRACLE

W hen a woman is pregnant, her body disposition takes on a different shape. She begins to experience life differently, even her eating habits change. In other to protect the baby, she becomes conscious of her environment and more careful with the company she keeps and how she exacts energy. After child birth, life takes on a new meaning, and new responsibilities emerge as she begins to live in two worlds. She condescends and relates to the level of the baby's world and at the same time nurturing the baby to grow up into the real world for fulfilment. Similarly, the miracle of the new birth is when a man is born again; he confesses Jesus as Lord and gives his heart to God. He is like the pregnant woman whose approach to life must change as he renounces his old ways and begins to walk in the newness of life. He ascribes to be like his maker which means that everything about his disposition now embraces this new way of living because of the change process from within that has taken root in his spirit-man. His approach and focus to life is now being redirected to conform to the new life he has received of the One whom he has believed. He no longer conforms to the old habit and the dictates of the world system, but renews his mind on a daily basis with prayer and the light of the glorious gospel of Christ which is the word of God. This informs and infers that human existence is of two dimensions; which invariably mean we live in two worlds, and must be careful how we trade the path of life if we're to gain eternal redemption; be complete and made every wit whole in God.

> *"And be not conformed to this world: but be ye transformed by the renewing of your mind..." (Romans 12: 2).*

> *"For though we walk in the flesh, we do not war after the flesh" (2 Corinthian 10: 3).*

Yes, we live in this world, but our existence is not measured by the standards and dictates of this world's system of doing things. To fully comprehend the new birth experience therefore, these scriptures are simply letting us know that at the primary stage, the spirit man of the new birth puts on a reformation, after which, a transformation process sets in because he has renounced his old ways and no longer lives by the dictates of his flesh, or systems of the world. Therefore, as a new man renewed in the spirit, the new birth helps to look beyond the immediate to the hopeful through the eyes of faith in the spoken word of God. This surmises that although we live in the world, we're not of the world since we've been chosen out of the world which is why our Lord Jesus said:

> [16]*Ye have not chosen me, but I have chosen you, and ordained you, that ye should go and bring forth fruit, and that your fruit should remain...* [18]*If the world hate you, ye know that it hated me before it hated you.* [19]*If ye were of the world, the world would love his own: but because ye are not of the world, but I have chosen you out of the world, therefore the world hateth you (John 15: 16, 18-19).*

CHUCKS UZONWANNE

This is the reason we do not conform to the things of the world knowing we're regenerated by the Spirit of the word of God which is the miracle of the new birth that has translated us into the kingdom of God through his dear Son, Jesus Christ. We are now born of the Spirit of God himself and no longer conform to the dictates of the world's system. Now that we're renewed in our inner-man and are made able to see life differently from the perspective of God helps us to embrace our focus on God as we're transformed in our spirit to think and do things according to the dictates of God's perfect will through the agency of his Holy Spirit. This explains the reason God's Spirit bears witness with our spirit that we're now the sons of God.

> [1]Behold, what manner of love the Father hath bestowed upon us, that we should be called the sons of God: therefore the world knoweth us not, because it knew him not. [2]Beloved, now are we the sons of God, and it doth not yet appear what we shall be: but we know that, when he shall appear, we shall be like him; for we shall see him as he is (1 John 3: 1-2).

What is new birth?

The miracle of the new birth is simply to be born again. To be translated from the kingdom of darkness to God's marvellous light. It means to be born of the Spirit and of water. This means you're born of the Holy Spirit and of the word of God.

> "[3]Jesus answered and said unto him, verily, verily, I say unto thee, except a man be born again; he cannot see the kingdom of God. [4]Nicodemus saith unto him, how can a man be born when he is old? Can he enter the second time into his mother's womb, and be born? [5]Jesus answered, Verily, verily, I say unto thee, except a man be

born of water and of the Spirit, he cannot enter into the kingdom of God. [6]That which is born of the flesh is flesh; and that which is born of the Spirit is spirit" (John 3: 3-6).

This new birth is further explained thus:

"Being born again not of corruptible seed, but of the incorruptible seed, by the word of God which liveth and abideth forever" (1 Peter 1: 23).

You see, when you're born again, unless you're baptized with the Holy Spirit, you will not truly understand who you are and your walk with the Father will not be as intimately real as it should be because as yet, he is not dwelling in you. Although he is with you, it becomes difficult for you to hear him and know in what direction he wants you to go, not being led by his Spirit. This is because your senses are still very much in control of you. But, the minute you're baptized with the Holy Spirit in the name of the Lord Jesus, the eyes of your understanding gets enlightened to hear and know God's direction for your life. For instance, the disciples of Jesus never understood his sayings until they were breathed upon by Jesus and the Holy Spirit (John 20: 22; see also 7: 39; Act 2: 38 - 9; 8: 15 - 17; 19: 1 - 6). This breath from God will enliven the word of God in your heart and make it become spirit and alive, and meaningfully gain residency in your spirit with revelation knowledge for you to bear witness to the voice of God's Spirit that you now hear. Another instance, when you're born again; what you've done is merely accent the Lordship of Jesus into your life which is good, but you need much more than that (Luke: 24: 44 - 49; Acts 3: 19; 8: 12 - 17; 22: 14 - 16). At this point, you're like someone who newly got introduced to a friend, just like in the case of the mother and the newly born baby, you both need to spend time together and get to know each other better.

CHUCKS UZONWANNE

This means you'll both share your thoughts on issues of interest which makes prayer very important to fan the fire of your intimacy. You might even talk about colours and other relevant things such as your likes and dislikes and many other interesting subjects that will help to get both of you acquainted intimately. You may even laugh and cry together sharing each other's feelings because you're now friends and care for one another.

In the same way, when you're born again, you receive the miracle of the new life that translate and introduces you into the kingdom. Now that you're in the kingdom, you need a companion; a guardian; you need the Holy Spirit to lead you and show you things to come. The Bible says,

> "*15If ye love me, keep my commandments. 16And I will pray the Father, and he shall give you another Comforter, that he may abide with you forever; 17Even the Spirit of truth; whom the world cannot receive, because it seeth him not, neither knoweth him: but ye know him; for he dwelleth with you, and shall be in you...26But the Comforter, which is the Holy Ghost, whom the Father will send in my name, he shall teach you all things, and bring all things to your remembrance, whatsoever I have said unto you" (John 14: 15-17, 26).*

Now that you're born again, the word of God reveals and relates the do's and don'ts of the kingdom. And by the leading of the Holy Spirit, as you begin to adhere to the instructions of the kingdom of God and do what the word says you'll be able to know how to be led by the Holy Spirit, and what to do in every given situation and how you're to do it. This helps you to know how to maintain an intimacy with God through prayer by telling him how you feel; listening, hearing and discerning his voice inorder to follow his instructions and do his perfect will. This infers that you need an intimacy with God to effectively pray and walk with him. For instance, someone who is learning to drive a car for the first time must take instructions from an instructor on how to start the car, hold the steering, and know the foot pedals; when to accelerate and when to apply the brakes. He needs to know how to turn on the indicators, change the gears, and keep his focus on the road. All of these will not be taught in one lesson; he will need sessions and hands-on practice before he can be perfected. These and other basic things are vital before he can then navigate his way through a busy road unto the high way by the leading of the instructor. Ironically, he may have the keys to the car and even occupy the driver's seat, but that doesn't mean he knows what to do or how to drive the car until he is shown the basic and necessary things he needs to know as a beginner up until he is certified able to drive. So is someone who is newly born again; he has been born into the kingdom all right, but he needs someone who knows, who understands and can navigate the way of the kingdom to show him what to do. Similarly, he needs the Holy Spirit to guide, lead and direct him when he prays. This means there is a process and a procedure he must adhere to for insight and for revelation knowledge that will help him to pray effectively and receive answers when he prays. At this stage, you need to realise that your spiritual ear and the eyes of your understanding will first have to be enlightened for you to insightfully comprehend spiritual verities for the Spirit of God to lead you.

> *"13Howbeit when he, the Spirit of truth, is come, he will guide you into all truth: for he shall not speak of himself; but whatsoever he shall hear, that shall he speak: and he will shew you things to come. 14He shall glorify me: for he shall receive of mine, and shall shew it unto you"* (John 16: 13-14).

CHUCKS UZONWANNE

Notice that it is at the point when you love Jesus and obey his commandments that the Spirit of truth comes. That is when the Holy Spirit comes to abide in you and be with you. He doesn't stop there; his intent is to lead and guide you into all truth as he hears from the Father, and to show you things to come. This means the Holy Spirit is revelatory in nature as he teaches and brings all things to your remembrance; and will show you things that are yet to come. For you to have this level of intimacy with the Father, of necessity, you must be born again, filled with the Holy Spirit, tongue talking and prayer loving.

> "*17Wherefore be ye not unwise, but understanding what the will of the Lord is. 18And be ... filled with the Spirit*" (Ephesians 5: 17-18).

The miracle of the new birth is to be born again. It is the entry passport of every believer in Christ into the kingdom of God the Father. In other words, the new birth means to have eternal life, the God kind of life through Christ Jesus.

> "*Jesus saith unto him, I am the way, the truth, AND THE LIFE: no man cometh unto the Father, but by me*" (John 14: 6).

This is that life in a human person that tells him apart from others because he is now born of God. He has right standing with God, and walks in holiness being led by God's Spirit. It also means you have been set apart for God to indwell and have become his headquarters through which he demonstrates the character of his Holy Presence. And because you carry the presence of God on the inside of you; you now have the ability to create an atmosphere of miracles wherever you go.

"For in him we live, and move, and have our being...
For we are also his offspring" (Acts 17: 28).

According to Concise Oxford English Dictionary, a miracle means
an extraordinary and welcome event that is not explicable by natural
or scientific laws, attributed to a divine agency. Invariably, it is a
wonderful supernatural occurrence considered to be the work of God.
An example is the existence of 'life.'

What is life?

Life is the breath of the Spirit of God in man known as breath or
wind. It is the force in a human being that determines its state of being
alive. It is an earth duration during which a living organism exists or
functions. This condition distinguishes animals, plants from inorganic
matter, including the capacity for growth, functional activity, and
continual change preceding death.

With these observations, it is easily deducible and evidently
conclusive that life stems from a supreme source which no natural
or scientific laws can prove making it a miracle. No science,
medicine or doctor can explain the formation of life. Life is an
inexplicable, extraordinary and a wonderfully supernatural work
of the Supreme Being generically known as 'God.' This further
explains why the Bible stamps a seal of claim when God declared
in *Ezekiel 18:4,*

"Behold, all souls are mine; as the soul of the father, so
also the soul of the son is mine..."

The Bible further correlates this statement in Isaiah 42: 5 thus:

"⁵Thus saith God the LORD, he that created the
heavens, and stretched them out; he that spread forth the
earth, and that which cometh out of it; he that giveth

breath unto the people upon it, and spirit to them that walk therein."

In the beginning, God having created the heavens and the earth, formed man out of the dust of the ground and breathed into his nostrils the breath of life and man became a living soul. And God said unto him to be fruitful and multiply. Notice that God made just one man and asked him to be fruitful and multiply; to replenish the earth and to subdue it. Consequently, man in the circle of life has evolved in the 21st century. Today, there are over 7 billion people on the face of the earth. This is a journey that began with just an individual, as a result, reveals the patient perseverance borne of the vision of the Supreme Being 'God'; the Almighty Creator who made all things and found them to be good.

How did God create life and why is mankind important in the circle of life? The bible gives us insight thus:

> *"26And God said, Let us make man in our image, after our likeness: and let them have dominion over the fish of the sea, and over the fowl of the air, and over the cattle, and over all the earth, and over every creeping thing that creepeth upon the earth. 27So God created man in his own image, in the image of God created he him; male and female created he them. 28And God blessed them, and God said unto them, be fruitful, and multiply, and replenish the earth, and subdue it" (Genesis 1: 26-28, see also Genesis 1: 11 – 12 & 9: 1 & 7).*

> *And the LORD God formed man of the dust of the ground, and breathed into his nostrils the breath of life; and man became a living soul (Genesis 2: 7).*

This insightfully reveals that life is from God and the importance of man in the circle of life is because God made man in his image and gave him dominion over all things. God formed man from the dust of the earth, and breathed into him the breath of life. This also implies that man is the breath of God (Psalm 82: 6 see also Ezekiel 18: 4). God blessed man whom he made and gave the control of the earth to him so he can be fruitful, and multiply and to replenish the earth, and subdue it. It also reveals that God is indeed patient which further explains the reason he has appointed a day in which he will bring judgment on all disobedient souls.

> "...For it is appointed unto man once to die and after death comes judgment" (Hebrews 9: 27).

The account of how man came into the picture of God's creation is a fascinating one. It is especially fascinating because it engages our attention as we go through the motion of creation, and are made to discover that in the beginning when God created the heavens and the earth, the earth was perceived to be a chaotic mass with darkness looming over the face of its depth and something remarkable happened. The power of prayer was unleashed and a wondrous episode of creation was revealed. And this revelation hallowed the introduction of the Supreme Being as he stepped into the picture gallery of creation with his Almighty Presence, and as he began to paint and to frame the earth, he recreated it in a canvass of wonder; a marvel of colours and a miracle of different species.

> "11And God said, Let the earth bring forth grass, the herb yielding seed, and the fruit tree yielding fruit after his kind, whose seed is in itself, upon the earth: and it was so. 12And the earth brought forth grass, and herb yielding seed after his kind, and the tree yielding fruit, whose seed was in itself, after his kind: and God saw that it was good...20And God said, Let the waters bring

CHUCKS UZONWANNE

forth abundantly the moving creature that hath life, and fowl that may fly above the earth in the open firmament of heaven. ²¹And God created great whales, and every living creature that moveth, which the waters brought forth abundantly, after their kind, and every winged fowl after his kind: and God saw that it was good. ²²And God blessed them, saying, Be fruitful, and multiply, and fill the waters in the seas, and let fowl multiply in the earth" (Genesis 1: 11-12, 20-22).

When God stepped in his creative presence stepped in with the power of prayer. One important cognitive thing is that the word 'God' is pluralised and his creative presence is the presence of the 'Holy Spirit and the Word.' The Bible further unveils this incredible insight as follows:

"AND GOD SAID; LET US make man in our image, after our likeness..." (Genesis 1: 26).

"¹In the beginning God created the heaven and the earth. ²And the earth was without form, and void; and darkness was upon the face of the deep. AND THE SPIRIT OF GOD MOVED upon the face of the waters. ³AND GOD SAID, Let there be light: and there was light" (Genesis 1: 1-3).

The first thing that was introduced at the beginning of creation was 'Elohim', and further to that there is a revelation that need be recognised. With its cognition the summary of the power of prayer can be deduceably understood. Listen once more and this time try to comprehend it,

"...and the Spirit of God moved upon the face of the waters..." (Genesis 1: 2).

I can perceive a question welling up within you. You are wondering how the Spirit of God can be upon the face of the waters and you're thinking to yourself and asking *'what does he mean'?* I need you to understand that God is Spirit and what this implies is that the Holy Spirit's Presence began to think on what to do to the chaotic mass of darkness, reason being that the Holy Spirit is the doer of God's word. In other words, the Spirit of God began to think, meditate; brood and ponder on what to do to change the hopeless situation and at God's ready time when he spoke, the Holy Spirit went into action to incubate and garnish light by the power of the spoken word and brought it to fruition because he is light. When you ingest these truths and settle it in your heart that the Holy Spirit is the doer of God's spoken word, this will inform the proclivity [tendency, propensity, inclination] of your perception to comprehend the thoughts of God at the point of his meditation and interestingly, it will further help you to fathom the need to always pray by applying the Spirit of the word of God.

The precedence of the power of prayer is the prayer of faith that activates the Spirit of God's word and puts it in motion through the agency of the Holy Spirit. This means, when you stand before God in prayer, your faith does not reckon with conditions and situations; it can only respond to the word of God and act in consonance to what the word says.

This is what makes the chaotic situation at the beginning of creation wonderful because it reveals the power of prayer as unleashed by God's meditative utterance. Letting us know that the concept of the power of prayer is the perceived awareness of the spoken word in faith. The interesting thing is that God had to look inward to conceptualise by seeking for a solution from within, and at the fullness of time, he spoke forth and light came by the power of his meditation. This is the power of prayer and it is through the agency of his creative presence known as the

Holy Spirit. Remember, God had to look inwards; now when God looked inward; God was communing in meditation. He was praying however, to no one else but himself. This motivation brought forth creation and thenceforth, God began to call forth the things of his meditation that were not as though they did already exist. Notice that God had to speak after looking inward before existence came into being. This agrees and alludes to the fact that there is a time and place to strategise in prayer and a time to decree proclaiming words of power. This further reveals that you cannot speak without first looking inward, that is, to reflectively pray. Invariably, you need the word of God if you are to rightly and effectively pray too.

Now, the earth is teeming with life and they were all good in the sight of God because the encapsulation of the power of prayer in meditation at God's verbalisation and declaration brought them forth into existence. And at the instance when God thought of making man, the power of creation took a different dimension, and the role of mankind was applauded by all creature standing astute beholding the entrance of man as God reproduced himself in the earth suit called 'man' making life a reality, with the intent for man to have dominion over all his created works.

> "²⁶And God said, Let us make man in our image, after our likeness: and let them have dominion over the fish of the sea, and over the fowl of the air, and over the cattle, and over all the earth, and over every creeping thing that creepeth upon the earth. ²⁷So God created man in his own image, in the image of God created he him; male and female created he them. ²⁸And God blessed them, and God said unto them, Be fruitful, and multiply, and replenish the earth, and subdue it: and have dominion over the fish of the sea, and over the fowl of the air, and over every living thing that moveth upon the earth" (Genesis 1: 26-28).

This insightful exegesis [interpretation] reveals that in the entire creation, none is like man. The beauty of creation was made complete and perfect when man was introduced and stepped onto the scene. The stage light of authority and dominion was beamed on mankind and his prominence was eminently established in that the power of prayer was conspicuously in the manner of speaking standing out evident. Whatever Adam called a thing was given the seal of approval by 'Jehovah' the Father of all spirits creator and maker of all things.

> "*19And out of the ground the LORD God formed every beast of the field, and every fowl of the air; and brought them unto Adam to see what he would call them: and whatsoever Adam called every living creature that was the name thereof. 20And Adam gave names to all cattle, and to the fowl of the air, and to every beast of the field*" (Genesis 2: 19-20).

PRAYER EXERCISE

1. What is the miracle of the new birth?
The miracle of the new birth is simply to be born again. To be translated from the kingdom of darkness to God's marvellous light. It means to be born of the Spirit and of water.

2. With what do you renew your mind?

_____

_____

3. How do you renew your mind?

_____

_____

4. Which of these scripture is best suitable
for renewing your mind?
(a) Romans 12: 2 (b) 2 Corinthians
10: 3 (c) Romans 10: 9 - 10

5. What is life?
Life is the breath of the Spirit of God in man known as breath or wind. It is the force in a human being that determines its state of being alive. It is an earth duration during which a living organism exists or functions. This condition distinguishes animals, plants from inorganic matter, including the capacity for growth, functional activity, and continual change preceding death.

CHAPTER EIGHT

THE SECRET OF PRAYER

God loves it when we pray because prayer is a sacred channel through which he blesses his children. He is the God of faith who desires our prosperity and success and his intent is for us to live in strength and in divine health. He wants us to be strong and courageous even in the face of opposition knowing our trust in him is all that's required to overcome seeming challenges. He wants to meet your needs and your communion with him in prayer is what helps your meditation and strengthens your faith to believe in what you're praying about for its manifestation. The secret of prayer is to believe you will receive what you're praying about and to trust in God's existence that he's the source from where your prayer request is granted. In other words, your confidence in God when you pray is predicated on the knowledge that you hail from him and must look to him as the source of your existence and benevolent provider. This infers when you pray in faith according to his will (1 John 5: 14 – 15); God hears and will always answer because his desire is to meet you at the point of your need according to his riches in glory by Christ Jesus (Philippians 4: 19). *Why does God desire for our needs to be met?* This is because he is our source who has promised to meet all our needs. This enables him to use the prayers of the saints to judge consequences on earth and change hopeless situations. And also reveals a level of spiritual responsibility vested in man that makes mankind very important in the circle of life.

The importance of man in the circle of life

- *Man is important in the completion of the circle of life because he is the only creature that is designed to be like his maker.*
- *Man was given dominion over all creation and vested with the responsibility to tend and keep the garden called earth.*
- *He was blessed by his maker to be fruitful, to multiply, to replenish and to subdue the earth.*

Above all creatures, man is endowed with authority to speak forth like his maker and bring the non-existent into existence, and this is accomplished through the power of prayer. *Why through Prayer?* This is because with prayer you can look inward within you and unleash tremendous power as did God at the beginning of creation. Also, with prayer you establish an intimate relationship with God that will make you exude confidence and know he is able to do exceeding, abundantly above all that you may ask or think according to his mighty power [ability] which is at work in you.

There is the ability of God in you waiting to be unleashed through the power of prayer so you can bring transformation to your world. This enablement is the unveiling of the secret of prayer which makes you the light of the world. It infers that in adverse and chaotic situations, you can awaken that fundamental intrinsic innate essential and inherent mighty power to speak forth in the name of the Lord and change any hopeless situation. And this can only be achieved through reflective thinking known as the power of prayer.

[17]Elias was a man subject to like passions as we are and he prayed earnestly that it might not rain: and it rained not on the earth by the space of three years and six months. [18]And he prayed again, and the heaven gave rain, and the earth brought forth her fruit (James 5: 17-18) (See also 1 kings 17: 1 & 18: 42-45).

This is what is known as the prayer of faith! When you have discovered and understood the secret of the power of prayer, you will know indeed that it is powerful people that pray a simple prayer to the powerful God. *How?* Elijah epitomised this when he prayed earnestly, revealing a heart-felt prayer of faith that makes tremendous power available. This is so in that prayer is more of a relationship with the one to whom you are praying than just asking for your needs to be met. This intimate relationship is established when you live and seek God for who he is in righteousness and in holiness. These righteous declarations are expectations predicated on the premise that God is who he says he is. And will meet all your needs without reservation because he knows what you need and when to meet them.

"...for your Father knoweth what things ye have need of, before ye ask him (Matthew 6: 8).

And just like God asked, sought and opened the doors of creation with prayer by looking inwards and calling forth those things that were not in existence as though they already existed; in like manner, he empowers you to do likewise. Our Lord Jesus used this allusion to teach on prayer and with it enjoins us saying,

"[7]Ask and it shall be given you; seek, and ye shall find; knock and it shall be opened unto you: [8]For every one that asketh receiveth; and he that seeketh findeth; and to him that knocketh it shall be opened. [9]Or what man is there of

you, whom if his son ask bread, will he give him a stone?
¹⁰Or if he ask a fish, will he give him a serpent? ¹¹If ye then,
being evil, know how to give good gifts unto your children,
how much more shall your Father which is in heaven give
good things to them that ask him? (Mathew 7: 7-11).

That you comprehend this scripture is to have at your finger tip 'the secret of the power of prayer.' This is the summary of the 'how-to of prayer' that you have been waiting for. To *'Ask... seek...knock'*, you may need a further revelation to fathom the depth of what this is saying if you would spend some quality time to contemplate on it prayerfully. This will help you gain more insight that will put you over and above all your troubles and also empower you to understand clearly the concept of communing with the Father in prayer.

It is until you come to the place of this intimacy which gives birth to deep spiritual revelations and understanding would you insightfully know that when you *'ask'* you are praying, when you *'seek'* you are praying and when you *'knock'* you are also praying. This is because everyone who asks receives, to him that seeks, finds, and to him who knocks, the doors of their destiny are opened for them to walk in victory and in dominion, in strength and in divine health.

God desires for you to be of sound mind and to succeed in your endeavour which explains for the need to pray always. As a matter of fact, there is a nudging for a revelation in my spirit as we speak. *Did you know that only powerful people pray a simple prayer to the powerful God? Are you lost and wondering what I mean?* There are three things that must be understood and clarified in this instance and they are:

- That 'powerful people' pray! *What makes them powerful?* Interestingly, it is because they commune regularly in prayer with the Father in the name of Jesus thereby contacting and contracting that same Spirit that rose up Christ Jesus from the dead (Romans 8: 11). Secondly, he has instilled in them the authority to speak and bring to fruition. This means that powerful people that pray are those who know their God and are strong enough to do exploit in his name (Daniel 11: 32; see also Micah 5: 9). This is because they spend quality time without ceasing in meditation and the study of the word serves as pedestal for their intimacy with the One to whom they relate to in prayer.

Their regular deep spirited and intimate fellowship with God inspires confidence and strength for exploits and brings about the discovery of their true identity in Christ. This makes them powerful people and puts in their hands the authority to decree a thing in faith and see it established (see also Matthew 18: 18).

- A 'simple prayer'! This doesn't necessarily have to be repetitive and long. It can be few words but dynamic with power and precision. This is why it can only be powerful people who pray this kind of simple prayer to the powerful God because they make tremendous power available whenever they pray in the name of Jesus Christ. What's important is for you to have faith and believe that God's word will not return void. This makes the word of God from your mouth sharper than any two-edged sword, and like the good marks man's arrow it does not miss its target. Our Lord Jesus said:

⁷But when ye pray, use not vain repetitions, as the heathen do: for they think that they shall be heard for their much speaking. ⁸Be not ye therefore like unto them: for your Father knoweth what things ye have need of, before ye ask him (Matthew 6: 7-8).

In other words, always ask with precision. Be precise, exact and specific. This will help you to be expectant and to receive because your Father in heaven loves you and knows what things you have need of and desires for you to have them. This further explains irrespective of situations the reason your expectation as a believing child of God will not be cut off!

- The dynamism of God! God is manifold in disposition and this makes him 'the Powerful God.' It becomes expedient to use an inference at this instance to illustrate the authority and unlimited power that makes God Omnipotent. For example, no good parents would be happy to see their children begging on the streets. Therefore, no parent would undermine their child when he's in trouble or crying for attention. *Or would you?* No, I don't think so. This makes it imperatively clear that you'll quickly race to the rescue of your child, and to know why he is crying. In the same manner, your heavenly Father hears when you cry out to him in prayers and knows it's in your best interest that he answers which is why the Bible says, *"...for your Father knoweth what things ye have need of before ye ask him..."* *(Matthew 6: 8).* Further to this, God knows when it's best for you to have it because he makes all things beautiful in his time and causes them to work together for your good. This demands diligence and patient perseverance in prayer which helps you develop an intimacy that will in return yield exceeding and abundant reward from God.

All of these reveal that our God is powerfully limitless because he is the Almighty, having infinite power and authority; infinite insight and knowledge.

This makes him Omnipotent because he can be wherever he chooses and is more than able to bring about our desires as he wills because he is Omniscient. This means that distance is not a barrier to him even if you are in the belly of a fish like Jonah; God is all powerful and more than able to save to the uttermost.

> ^{1} *Then Jonah prayed unto the LORD his God out of the fish's belly...* ^{10}*And the LORD spake unto the fish, and it vomited out Jonah upon the dry land (Jonah 2: 1 & 10).*

This shows that regardless of your situation or where you are presently in life; God is more than willing to hear your cry and come to your rescue if you will trust and call on him this minute. You could be in the hospital right now or innocently in prison like Joseph or Peter. You could be under rubble of the earth or swallowed by a fish like Jonah. It doesn't matter the challenges you're facing right now or how bad things are with you, just call to him for he is waiting to hear from you and more importantly, he is more than willing to answer you because he is more than able to meet all your needs. Hear once again what the Bible says of him:

> *"And now unto him that is able to do exceeding abundantly above all that we may ask or think according to his mighty power which is at work in you" (Ephesians 3: 20; see also Matthew 21: 21 - 22).*

It is therefore inevitably evident that powerful people who pray a simple prayer to the powerful God are those who exercise their faith and have discovered their true identity. They know whose they are and the authority they have been vested with because of the power of prevailing prayer that's at work in them. Also, they being led by the Spirit of God are vested with authority that enables them to speak, proclaiming the word of God in power as they decree in the name of Jesus Christ.

Does it mean that not everybody is led by God's Spirit and has the authority to speak in his name?

Absolutely, yes! This is the exact reason, when you pray; you must do so with the knowledge and understanding of who you are in Christ and what the word of God is saying concerning what you are praying about. This makes prayer for those who pray with knowledge of the word of God and the understanding of the authority they have in Christ excitingly simple because they know that as long as they are praying the right way God will always hear and answer them.

With this inference it is imperatively obvious there is the right way to pray; and those who pray the right way are those who have come to the place of knowledge where their fellowship with God have gone *beyond 'O God, give me this, give me that', to 'Lord, what would you have me do today?'* Assuredly, those whose mind-set is of the latter are powerful praying people who masticate strong meat and bones. These are worthy ambassadors of Christ who have come to maturity and have the ministry of reconciliation. Their intent is to bring transformation by injecting spiritual life into the destiny of those they come in contact with. They love to demonstrate the character of the Spirit of God as sons of God who acknowledge the authority they have in the name of Jesus Christ as they make things happen wherever they go. And because they are led by God's Spirit, they know how, when and where the Spirit leads just like Philip who was a man of the Spirit. Let's learn from him that we may give heed to the voice of the Spirit of God and be relevant in the kingdom.

> *[26]And the angel of the Lord spake unto Philip, saying, Arise, and go toward the south unto the way that goeth down from Jerusalem unto Gaza, which is desert. [27]And he arose and went: and, behold, a man of Ethiopia, an eunuch of great authority under Candace queen of the Ethiopians, who had the charge of all her treasure, and had come to Jerusalem for to worship, [28]Was returning, and sitting in his chariot read Esaias the prophet. [29]Then*

*the Spirit said unto Philip, Go near, and join thyself to
this chariot. ³⁰And Philip ran thither to him, and heard
him read the prophet Esaias, and said, understandeth
thou what thou readest? ³¹And he said, How can I, except
some man should guide me? And he desired Philip that
he would come up and sit with him. ³²The place of the
scripture which he read was this, He was led as a sheep to
the slaughter; and like a lamb dumb before his shearer, so
opened he not his mouth:*

*³³In his humiliation his judgment was taken away:
and who shall declare his generation? For his life is taken
from the earth. ³⁴And the eunuch answered Philip, and
said, I pray thee, of whom speaketh the prophet this? Of
himself, or of some other man? ³⁵Then Philip opened his
mouth, and began at the same scripture, and preached unto
him Jesus. ³⁶And as they went on their way, they came unto
certain water: and the eunuch said, See, here is water;
what doth hinder me to be baptized? ³⁷And Philip said,
If thou believest with all thine heart, thou mayest. And he
answered and said, I believe that Jesus Christ is the Son of
God. ³⁸And he commanded the chariot to stand still: and
they went down both into the water, both Philip and the
eunuch; and he baptized him. ³⁹And when they were come
up out of the water, the Spirit of the Lord caught away
Philip, that the eunuch saw him no more: and he went on
his way rejoicing. ⁴⁰But Philip was found at Azotus: and
passing through he preached in all the cities, till he came
to Caesarea (Acts 8: 26-40).*

*Can you now see that it is because Philip was a powerful praying
man, an ambassador of the gospel of Christ that he was able to hear
the voice of the Spirit and also led by the Spirit of God?* You need
the power of prayer; you need to be full of the word of God,
filled with the Spirit and the ability to witness the gospel of our

Lord and Saviour Jesus Christ before you can be led by the Holy Spirit of God. *What do I mean?* For you to be led by the Spirit of God; you must resolve to carry your cross on a daily basis and separate yourself unto God by making prayer a prioritised life style, witnessing the gospel of Christ just like Philip obeyed the injunctions of our Lord and Saviour Jesus Christ. You must let it be your heart beat if you are to excel with God like Apostle Paul.

By ceaselessly soaking yourself in prayer and the study of the word of God, you open yourself to a myriad of intimate fellowship with Jehovah 'the prayer answering God.' This will bring about your spiritual promotion and cause you to find fulfilment in life. It will help you to understand the essence of the inherent nature of the power of prayer as it opens for you an array of knowledge on how to pray the God-way and apply the word of God accurately for results. Also, the Spirit of God himself will regularly prop you up and stir in you the hunger to pray and intercede for others.

The power that lies behind our praying cannot be easily understood until we come to the place of the knowledge of the word of God. This will help us to appreciate the importance and place of prayer for which God desires for every believer so he can answer their prayer and reveal supernatural things that would help them structure their lives in righteousness and live holy. With this, the believer will further understand who he is, the authority he has, what is expected of him, and the limitless power that is at work in him. It is because Apostle Paul understood the place of prayer as a result of his relationship with the powerful prayer answering God that made him declare to the Ephesians church:

> *"Now unto him that is able to do exceeding abundantly above all that we ask or think, according to the power that worketh in us" (Ephesians 3:20).*

This is saying that God is more than able to do according to his power that is at work in you. There is the power at work in you if only you will look inward, and this is the power of prayer engineered by the ability of God that resides in you. This can also be discovered and revealed when you go on a spiritual journey by separating yourself to the study of the word of God, and immersing yourself in Prayer and fasting.

For a journey of spiritual discovery of these sort, of necessity, the need for isolation, separating yourself from spiritual pollution and reaching out for a contemplative meditative prayer life which will inspire in you the ability to speak forth the word with power must be employed. These becomes words with the creative ability to reproduce its kind once it is decreed in the name of Jesus Christ because of the atmosphere created through prayer which ushers in God's holy presence.

Remember your fellowship with him creates an atmosphere of the miraculous and this happens due to your constant fellowshipping with the Holy Spirit. Don't forget that the Holy Spirit is the doer of God's word and responds to prayer made in the name of Jesus Christ. This is so because the Holy Spirit only answers to the name of Jesus Christ.

> *"BUT THE COMFORTER, WHICH IS THE HOLY GHOST, WHOM THE FATHER WILL SEND IN MY NAME, he shall teach you all things, and bring all things to your remembrance, whatsoever I have said unto you" (John 14: 26; see also John 15: 26, 16: 7, 13; 1 John 2: 27).*

CHUCKS UZONWANNE

PRAYER EXERCISE

1. What is the secret of prayer? See page 100

_____

_____

_____

2. Explain the importance of man in the circle of life?
(a) Man is important in the completion of the circle
of life because he is the only creature that
is designed to be like his maker.
(b) Man was given dominion over all creation
and vested with the responsibility to tend
and keep the garden called earth.
(c) He was blessed by his maker to be fruitful, to
multiply, to replenish and to subdue the earth.

CHAPTER NINE

THE PLACE OF PRAYER

The place of prayer is the place of grace, integration, and transformation. It is the place for aloneness and oneness with the Lord, where separating self from the world unites you with the Lord. The place of prayer is the place of the birthing of concepts; it is a place for discovering purpose and destiny because you're in consonance and in one accord with the Lord. This is where brokenness and total surrender, contemplation and expectation discover complete intimacy with the Lord now they're birthed in unity of purpose. This makes the place of prayer the place of power where you are filled with authority and ability from on high to change hopeless situations because the Holy Spirit imparts you with spiritual wisdom and inundates you with revelation knowledge, causing the eyes of your understanding to be enlightened so you can see and receive insight into spiritual verities that makes you to understand the things of the kingdom. The place of prayer is the place of great impartation of grace by the anointing of the Holy Spirit, where you find favour with all men; even your enemies become at peace with you because you're at peace with God and has favour with him.

³¹And when they had prayed, the place was shaken where they were assembled together; and they were all filled with the Holy Ghost, and they spake the word of God with

boldness. ³²And the multitude of them that believed were
of one heart and of one soul: neither said any of them that
ought of the things which he possessed was his own; but they
had all things common. ³³And with great power gave the
apostles witness of the resurrection of the Lord Jesus: and
great grace was upon them all (Acts 4: 31-33).

With this it becomes expedient to know the advantages of prayer since we're made to understand that prayer charts the believer's course and orchestrates his future granting him the fruit of the Spirit to live a fulfilled life in Christ Jesus. The pertinence of prayer can be seen in the above scripture that says,

> *"³¹And when they had prayed, the place was shaken*
> *where they were assembled together; and they were all filled*
> *with the Holy Ghost, and they spake the word of God with*
> *boldness...³³And with great power gave the apostles witness*
> *of the resurrection of the Lord Jesus: and great grace was*
> *upon them all" (Acts 4: 31&33).*

You need to understand that power was made available by the Holy Spirit when they prayed. This enabled the apostles to preach the word of God with boldness and the multitude who heard them believed, and great grace was giving to them all to function in love as those who believed were added to the number and none of them lacked anything. This is because great power went forth to convict the multitude as the apostles witnessed the resurrection of the Lord Jesus, and that enabled them with great grace to be of one heart and share their possessions in common. This makes it imperative for every believer to pray because:

- *Prayer helps you define the true meaning of love and fellowship, that is, love for God and to all mankind. This motivates you to witness the love of Christ to those in the hospital, the prison yard, your neighbourhood and people in your sphere of contact.*

- *Through prayer you can fellowship with the sick and visit the widows, the orphans and the less privileged to pray for them. Prayer grants and imparts you with the grace and knowledge to reconcile sinners back to God by enabling you with boldness to introduce them to Jesus.*

- *With prayer there is an accord in the realms of the spirit that brings about unity of purpose. When believers pray in one accord, God command his blessings and multiplies their increase.*

- *Prayer helps you to discover the gifts of the Spirit, your true calling and reveals your essence to know what God has called you to do in the body of Christ (1 Corinthians 12: 1 – 13).*

- *Prayer grants you focus and defines your perspective. This brings you peace even in the face of opposition because of whose you are. It defines your paradigm and helps you see things differently and further helps to establish your confidence in God (2 Kings 6).*

- *With prayer, you can have sound mind and live in divine health. If for any reason you are sick in your body, with constant prayer known as the prayer of faith, you can reverse and receive your healing, giving meaning to your life (James 5: 13 – 16).*

- *With prayer you can change any hopeless situation and bring prosperity and success into your life (Mark 11: 22 – 24).*

- *With prayer you can pull down strong holds and move any besieging mountain (2 Corinthians 10: 3 – 5; Ephesians 6: 10 – 18; Matthew 21: 21 - 22).*

- *With prayer you can change the course of a nation from destruction and gain victory over your enemies (3: 1 - 10; Daniel 9: 1 - 27; Ezekiel 28: 1 - 26; 2 Chronicles 20: 1 - 30).*

- *With prayer your joy will be full and abound and remain for your walk with God to be sweet. This makes the power*

CHUCKS UZONWANNE

of prayer the effectual fervent prayer of a righteous man that makes tremendous power avail much. There is power in prayer!

"4...And, being assembled together with them, commanded them that they should not depart from Jerusalem, but wait for the promise of the Father, which, saith he, ye have heard of me. 5For John truly baptized with water; but ye shall be baptized with the Holy Ghost not many days hence... 8But ye shall receive power, after that the Holy Ghost is come upon you: and ye shall be witnesses unto me both in Jerusalem, and in all Judaea, and in Samaria, and unto the uttermost part of the earth. 12Then returned they unto Jerusalem from the mount called Olivet, which is from Jerusalem a Sabbath day's journey. 13And when they were come in, they went up into an upper room, where abode both Peter, and James, and John, and Andrew, Philip, and Thomas, Bartholomew, and Matthew, James the son of Alphaeus, and Simon Zelotes, and Judas the brother of James. 14THESE ALL CONTINUED WITH ONE ACCORD IN PRAYER AND SUPPLICATION, with the women, and Mary the mother of Jesus, and with his brethren (Acts 1: 4, 5, 8, 12, 13, and 14).

Sequel to the previewed scriptures, you will deduce the following:

1. *The place of prayer is the place to wait on the Lord.*
2. *It is the place to be endued with power from on high.*
3. *It is a place to receive power after baptism.*
4. *And the place of prayer is a place wherefrom you are sent forth to witness Christ to all men.*

Here were the disciples of Jesus trying to get their acts together after Jesus had resurrected and showed himself to them on several occasions for forty days. Jesus knew for them to effectively carry out their obligation of preaching the gospel, they needed to be endued with power from on high. And here comes Jesus to reassure them that they all will be endued with the Holy Spirit if they tarry in Jerusalem for the work he has promised them. This lets us know that without the Holy Spirit their work would have been futile, fruitless, unproductive, unsuccessful and in vain. Their preaching would not have been effective nor would it have made an impact in the world because it would have lacked the dynamic ability to cause changes.

This is insightful in the sense that the Holy Spirit can only empower the word of God in you when mixed with obedience and regular prayer. This invariably is responsible for the reason the Bible says, *"It is not by power nor is it by might, but by my Spirit says the Lord"* *(Zachariah 4: 6).*

The Essence of the Holy Spirit

The Holy Spirit is the one who determines the place of prayer. He is the one who knows when it is time to empower and directs. This means that the Holy Spirit protects and orders the footsteps of believers and leads them in the paths of righteousness and holiness (Isaiah 52: 7; Romans 10: 15; Nahum 1: 15). The Holy Spirit energises the believer to witness Christ with power (Acts 1: 8; Luke 24: 49; Matthew 28: 18 - 20). This is because the Holy Spirit sanctifies and makes the word of God in your mouth to be immutable and efficacious to produce your desired result (Matthew 16: 19; 18: 18; John 20: 23). The Holy Spirit expresses the totality of God the Father in the name of Jesus. This is so because he responds to the name of Jesus and brings to fruition the words of Jesus. This means that whenever you call on the name of Jesus, the Holy Spirit comes from the Father; he hails and proceeds from the Father to represent the name of Jesus. You will get the full import of the Holy Spirit in my book titled *"The Elevation of* the Spirit" and "Strong Faith." This is where you get to know fully who the Holy Spirit is and why he responds to the name of Jesus.

In the scripture directly below, an introduction of one of the Holy Spirit's synonyms was given as the 'comforter' whom the Father will send in the name of Jesus. In other words, when the Holy Spirit comes to you, he comes to comfort, teach and bring all things spoken by Jesus to your remembrance:

> But the Comforter, which is the Holy Ghost [Spirit], whom the Father will send in my name, he shall teach you all things, and bring all things to your remembrance, whatsoever I have said unto you (John 14: 26).

Can you now see the reason the apostles were so bold even in the face of opposition to proclaim the word of God in the name of Jesus Christ with power. This is because they were endued by the Holy Ghost to function supernaturally. Jesus knew for them to receive this power they have to be where the Holy Spirit had chosen to meet with them. And so he:

> "...commanded them that they should not depart from Jerusalem, but wait for the promise of the Father, which, saith he...but ye shall be baptized with the Holy Ghost not many days hence..." (Acts 1: 5).

- The essence of the Holy Spirit is empowerment "...But ye shall receive power, after that the Holy Ghost is come upon you" (Acts 1: 8).
- Secondly, to witness the living word of God and reveal who Jesus is "...and ye shall be witnesses unto me..." (Acts 1: 8). Also, notice that all these comes as a result of prayer"...These all continued with one accord in prayer and supplication" (Acts 1: 14).

PRAYER EXERCISE

1. What is the place of prayer?
The place of prayer is the place of grace, integration, and transformation. It is a place for discovering purpose and destiny because you're in consonance and in one accord with the Lord. This is where brokenness and total surrender, contemplation and expectation discover complete intimacy with the Lord now they're birthed in unity of purpose.

2. In your own concept explain the place of prayer? See pages 112 - 114.

_____

_____

_____

3. Give 3 advantages of prayer? See pages 113 - 115

_____

_____

_____

4. What is the essence of the Holy Spirit? See page 116 - 117

_____

_____

5. Give 3 importance of the Holy Spirit? See page 116 - 117

_____

_____

_____

CHUCKS UZONWANNE

CHAPTER TEN

PRAYER: A WALK WITH GOD

"And when he had sent the multitudes away, he went up into a mountain apart to pray: and when the evening was come, he was there alone" (Matthew 14: 23).

I n all the synoptic gospel an excellent leadership examples where laid by our Lord Jesus Christ on prayer. As his habit was, this preview reveals how our Lord Jesus Christ set time aside to spend in the presence of God. He sought the face of God in all that he did. He walked with God through prayer. In the same manner, every believer is to follow the laudable examples of our Lord Jesus Christ and pray at all times. It is imperative that we receive direct guidance from the Lord in all our endeavours through prayer. This is because the essence of prayer is so the believer does not grow weary and lose hope:

> *³Simon Peter saith unto them, I go a fishing. They say unto him, we also go with thee. They went forth, and entered into a ship immediately; and that night they caught nothing. ⁴But when the morning was now come, Jesus stood on the shore: but the disciples knew not that it was Jesus. ⁵Then Jesus saith unto them, Children, have ye any meat? They answered him, No. ⁶And he said unto them, cast the*

net on the right side of the ship, and ye shall find. They
cast therefore, and now they were not able to draw it for
the multitude of fishes (John 21: 3-6).

However troubled the billowing sea; you do not give up on your destiny until you have achieved your God given purpose once you are called by God because Jesus the author, finisher and perfecter of your faith is standing on the shores of your destiny. There is no gain saying that there are times when challenges are so overwhelming that they seem endless like eternity, however if you will listen to the voice of Jesus, it will all turn around for your good. The disciples toiled all night and caught nothing; seldom did they know the Lord Jesus was standing at the sea shore until they heard the voice of Jesus, and in obedience enclosed a multitude of fishes. This suggests in overwhelming circumstances, you just want a way out, but giving up should not be an option. Instead of quitting, intensify efforts and cry to God for mercy, indulge yourself in meditative prayer, and keep on praying knowing that your life depends on it. Pray and keep on praying until something happens.

Look at Peter with the baton of leadership who was supposed to be exemplary, but when the situation became overwhelmingly difficult he led the other disciples away from their calling. They forsook their calling and went back to fishing and began to struggle. The Bible says, *"...that night they caught nothing..."* until our Lord Jesus got on the scene. Jesus is in that boat with you right now however boisterous the raging storm; he will not leave you forsaken. You may have lost your loved one or may be experiencing turbulence in your marriage, you may have just been made redundant at work; perhaps your 16 year old daughter came home pregnant with no man to claim responsibility or maybe your beloved son is with the wrong influence and has taken to drugs, whatever the unforeseen circumstance. If you will cast all these burdens upon Jesus and let him take charge over your life and be your Lord and Saviour; you will walk free because he who the Son make free is free indeed (John 8: 36; see also Matthew 11: 28).

Look up and cry to Jesus sincerely from a contrite heart and watch him turn it all around for your good. All you need is the power of prayer to hear and know in what direction he wants you to go and prevail. Like him, he was frequently concerned that his disciples pray habitually in order to accomplish God's purposes for their lives (Matthew 26: 41). You must also bear in mind that to faint is to give up or lose heart. He does not want us to fail or relent in our duties. All we need is the power of prayer.

> *"And he spake a parable unto them to this end, that men ought always to pray, and not to faint" (Luke 18: 1 see also 1 Thessalonians 5: 17).*

Do you know that prayer helps you to walk with God? This is why I'm telling you so you can understand that a walk with God is separation from the world. This infers that although you live in the world, you are not of the world system. This is because you exist and operate a higher law than that of the world. *What do I mean?* When a man is born again, he is born into God's kingdom where adherence to the laws of the Spirit of life must be fully observed. This means you now need to work out your salvation with reverence and humility by walking in consonance with the word of God and living a holy and righteous life. Further to these, you are to eschew all forms of evil as you put on God's full armour of righteousness.

> *"But put ye on the Lord Jesus Christ, and make not provision for the flesh, to fulfil the lusts thereof" (Romans 13: 14; Ephesians 6: 10 - 18).*

This enables you to live a holy life because God is holy (Leviticus 11: 44; 1 Peter 1: 15 - 16). What you need now that you're born again to help you walk effectively with God is the power of prayer.

What does prayer do? Prayer helps you to hear the audible voice of the spirit, and also to stir you in the right direction as you allow the Holy Spirit to lead and guide you. Prayer helps you worship God in spirit and in truth. With prayer established as a relationship, God desires for us to walk in righteousness and live in holiness because he loves us and wants us to operate on his level and in his terms now that we're born into his kingdom. Being born again is being born into God's family [kingdom], and having God's Spirit lead, guide, direct and indwell the believer through prayer. This means full compliance with, and adherence to the word of God. For example, if you have a house where you live, most probably you would expect every person who comes to live with you to adhere and abide by the laws that govern your home. That way you can identify with whomsoever is living with you otherwise, you would ask the fellow to leave your house because he or she does not respect your governance. Whosoever will live amicably in your house, must of necessity, abide by the rules and regulations that govern your house. In the same manner, although we are in the world, we are not of the world system because there are governing laws that binds us together with the one whom we are answerable to, and prayer helps us to keep our trust in him.

"And they continued stedfastly in the apostles' doctrine and fellowship, and in breaking of bread, and in PRAYERS" (Acts 2: 42; see also Romans 8: 2).

Your obedience and adherence to God's set rules will cause him to come to your rescue whenever you are in trouble and answer your prayers because those are his set rules and he cannot violate them (Psalm 50: 15; 91: 15; John 12: 26; 1 Samuel 2: 30).

CHUCKS UZONWANNE

So when you come before God in prayer; praying the patient and persevering, *"Grant me justice"* kind of prayer, that is the everyday never ceasing, unyielding and relentless kind of prayer known as the prayer of faith (Luke 18: 1-8); God will hear and come to your rescue because you're walking with him in obedience to his word by faith through prayer.

Your intimacy with him and obedience to his word will cause him to protect you from the clutches of your perpetrators, and make his favour rest upon you to overcome seeming challenges so you can walk in victory and in dominion, and have good success. Just like we said in the example above, there is a condition to all of these for which the Lord can be your Shepherd and not allow your feet to be removed. This condition is for you to obey the word of God with all your heart and soul, and to walk in righteousness and holiness. Your heart must be pure towards all men, do not be enviously jealous of people, do not think evil of others as a matter of fact, you are supposed to pray for those who despitefully use you and bless them that curse you; let God deal with them in their own coin:

> *"...But I say unto you, Love your enemies, bless them that curse you, do good to them that hate you, and pray for them which despitefully use you, and persecute you..."* *(Matthew 5: 44; Genesis 50: 19 -21; Genesis 45: 4 - 9; Leviticus 19: 18; Proverbs 20: 22; 24: 29; Deuteronomy 32: 35; Isaiah 34: 8; Romans 12: 17 – 20; Proverbs 17: 13, 15).*

God knew Peter was in trouble when Herod put him in prison, and this is because of the relationship Peter had developed with him through the power of prayer. Secondly, the prayers of the saints who were gathered in the house of Mary the mother of John Mark on behalf of Peter came before God in power, and so he quickly rescued Peter knowing Peter's assignment on earth was not yet over. If God had not intervened, Herod would have killed him like he killed James the brother of John:

> [1]Now about that time Herod the king stretched forth his hands to vex certain of the church. [2]And he killed James the brother of John with the sword. [3]And because he saw it pleased the Jews, he proceeded further to take Peter also. (Then were the days of unleavened bread). [4]And when he had apprehended him, he put him in prison, and delivered him to four quaternions of soldiers to keep him; intending after Easter to bring him forth to the people. [5]Peter therefore was kept in prison: BUT PRAYER WAS MADE WITHOUT CEASING OF THE CHURCH UNTO GOD FOR HIM. [6]And when Herod would have brought him forth, the same night Peter was sleeping between two soldiers, bound with two chains: and the keepers before the door kept the prison. [7]And, behold, the angel of the Lord came upon him, and a light shined in the prison: and he smote Peter on the side, and raised him up, saying, Arise up quickly. And his chains fell off from his hands. [8]And the angel said unto him, Gird thyself, and bind on thy sandals. And so he did. And he saith unto him, Cast thy garment about thee, and follow me. [9]And he went out, and followed him; and wist not that it was true which was done by the angel; but thought he saw a vision. [10]When they were past the first and the second ward, they came unto the iron gate that leadeth unto the city; which opened to them of his own accord: and they went out, and passed on through one street; and forthwith the angel departed from him. [11]And when Peter was come to himself, he said, NOW I KNOW OF A SURETY, THAT THE LORD HATH SENT HIS ANGEL, AND HATH DELIVERED ME OUT OF THE HAND OF HEROD, AND FROM ALL THE EXPECTATION OF THE

PEOPLE OF THE JEWS. ¹²*And when he had considered the thing, he came to the house of Mary the mother of John, whose surname was Mark; WHERE MANY WERE GATHERED TOGETHER PRAYING (Acts 12: 1-12).*

The driving force in the previewed scripture is the coming together of the believers who when they heard that Peter had been apprehended and put in prison by Herod, all of them put the power of prayer into motion by ceaselessly praying and interceding for Peter. Notice that he took James and killed him with the sword, seeing that it pleased the Jews, he proceeded and took Peter also, and these were the disciples of Jesus. If nothing had been done about Peter by they interceding for him and exercising the power of prayer, most probably he would have been killed the very next day by Herod to please the Jews also. There are factors we must take into consideration that helped to save the life of Peter:

- *All the believers came together and worked with God by exercising their faith through the power of prayer*
- *They had unity of purpose; they we're of one mind and in one accord*
- *They understood the importance of intercessory prayer*
- *They believed in the power of prayer*
- *They understood the ministry of intercession and applied it to their hopeless situation.*
- *They knew prayer is the inevitable key that reverses the irreversible*
- *They believed in the prayer answering God*
- *They understood prayer to be the key in the hand of faith that opens the door of destiny*

Because the believers stood in the gap in prayer for Peter, God heard their prayer. There is power in prayer and it is undisputable!

And so they prayed and prayed, and kept on praying until Peter's prison door was opened.

To reiterate there is power in prayer is not over-emphasizing it; there is power in prayer when it is borne of purpose. This means that every believer ought to always stand in the gap in prayer for the incarcerated innocent and less privileged who are victims in their own right. This also reveals that the power of prayer is made available to everyone who believes because God mysteriously uses our prayers to judge consequences. This is so because God hears our prayer even in times of trouble and desires to bring about our justice for his glory if we will not relent in our prayers. And so, the Bible enjoins to:

"Pray without ceasing" (1 Thessalonians 5: 17; see also Daniel 10: 2 - 14).

"Pray always with all prayer and supplication in the Spirit, and watching thereunto with all perseverance and supplication for all saints" (Ephesians 6: 18).

When a believer comes before God in prayer, purpose must be the driving force if the believer must prevail in prayer. With purpose at sight and in hand, the believer's prayer life must be ceaselessly regular. It is at the point when we serve God earnestly and continually that our prayer becomes effective and powerful. It is important that we must learn to pray believing at all times regardless of how we feel, what we see, what we hear that is opposed to our beliefs and what the present circumstances dictate. The believers who gathered in the house of Mary the mother of John Mark, although they had purpose in mind and interceded for Peter could not believe the immediate response they got when they were told that Peter was standing at the door. This is prove positive that someone might be praying for something, yet be in doubt as to the possibility of receiving an answer to his prayers.

CHUCKS UZONWANNE

This is the case with many praying believers who pray and yet are walking in unbelief.

Unbelief will nullify your prayer the minute you doubt that God will hear and answer. This will also put you in a deeper trouble because here you are praying alright but something is wrong because you are not getting answers. You are not getting answers because you are praying the wrong way in unbelief and cannot recognise the answer when it comes. If you find yourself in this category, I recommend that you get the book titled: **Faith for Increase: How to Exercise your Faith**. And to command confidence in your walk with God; get the book titled: **Having Confidence in God being Led by His Spirit**. Also, get the books titled: **Life Transforming Prayer and Strong Faith**. All of these books can be purchased online or at Christ House of Destiny Ministries or from the website: *www.pastorchucks.com*

As a matter of fact, the reason that challenges come to a believer most times is to test your faith. This is why I keep saying that faith thrives in the face of opposition. These are some of the reasons you need the recommended books to help boost your confidence and faith in God through prayer. Settle it in your heart that being positively confident in your prayers and immoveable in the face of troubles and opposition is the reassurance and prove that God is with you. For instance, after the killing of Steven the believers' faith were tried and this helped to influence the preaching and the spread of the gospel everywhere (Acts 6: 6 – chapter 8). Reason is because at that time there was a great persecution against the church which was at Jerusalem; and they were all scattered abroad throughout the regions of Judea and Samaria, except the apostles. If the church hadn't been persecuted, it would have taken the believers and the apostles a much longer time to accomplish the injunction given by Jesus for them to go into the entire world and preach the gospel (Matthew 28: 19; Mark 16: 15). This evidence reveal that sometimes God allows persecution and opposition as a wakeup call to move us from complacency to doing what is expected of us. Another instance is the story of Jacob:

> [9]And Jacob said, O God of my father Abraham, and God of my father Isaac, the LORD which saidst unto me, Return unto thy country, and to thy kindred, and I will deal well with thee: [10]I am not worthy of the least of all the mercies, and of all the truth, which thou hast shewed unto thy servant; for with my staff I passed over this Jordan; and now I am become two bands. [11]Deliver me, I pray thee, from the hand of my brother, from the hand of Esau: for I fear him, lest he will come and smite me, and the mother with the children. [12]And thou saidst, I will surely do thee good, and make thy seed as the sand of the sea, which cannot be numbered for multitude (Genesis 32: 9 – 12).

This conveys for us composures that *"when the ways of a man please the Lord; he makes even his enemies to be at peace with him"* (Proverbs 16: 7; see also Isaiah 26: 3 - 4).

A man could be in trouble; and because he is distressed and in great fear at that moment may not think of seeking the Lord in prayer particularly if he does not know how. That is when the adage that says *"The mystery of harmony and focus is peace"* eludes him because at that instance, there is no cordiality between the peace-giver and the one that is supposed to be seeking peace. However, when he surrenders his life completely to the Lord in that circumstance, and commits his ways entirely by making the Lord his Shepherd, he will make his enemies to be at peace with him. Jacob from his experience and encounters with his brother Esau and his uncle Laban, coupled with his encounter with God made him learn to seek God in answer to his troubles.

This lets us know that prayer is necessary in the time of trouble and ensures our relationship with God if we must have favour with men. Jacob felt his scheming sense knowledge would do it at first, so he proffered gifts to placate Esau but that didn't work; it didn't move Esau until Jacob surrendered to God in prayer. It was the power of prayer that subdued Esau with favour from God for Jacob. Another remarkable instance is when Abraham wanted a wife for his son Isaac that Abraham's servant had to pray when he got to Mesopotamia:

> "[10]Then the servant took ten of his master's camels and left, taking with him all kinds of good things from his master. He set out for Aram Naharaim - Mesopotamia and made his way to the town of Nahor. [11]He had the camels kneel down near the well outside the town; it was toward evening, the time the women go out to draw water. [12]THEN HE PRAYED, "O LORD, GOD OF MY MASTER ABRAHAM, GIVE ME SUCCESS TODAY, AND SHOW KINDNESS TO MY MASTER ABRAHAM. [13]SEE, I AM STANDING BESIDE THIS SPRING, AND THE DAUGHTERS OF THE TOWN'S PEOPLE ARE COMING OUT TO DRAW WATER. [14]MAY IT BE KNOWN THAT WHEN I SAY TO A GIRL, 'PLEASE LET DOWN YOUR JAR THAT I MAY HAVE A DRINK,' AND SHE SAYS, 'DRINK, AND I'LL WATER YOUR CAMELS TOO' – LET HER BE THE ONE YOU HAVE CHOSEN FOR YOUR SERVANT ISAAC. BY THIS I WILL KNOW THAT YOU HAVE SHOWN KINDNESS TO MY MASTER." [15]Before he had finished praying, Rebekah came out with her jar on her shoulder. She was the daughter of Bethuel son of Milcah, who was the wife of Abraham's brother Nahor. [16]The girl was very beautiful, a virgin; no man

had ever lain with her. She went down to the spring, filled her jar and came up again. *¹⁷The servant hurried to meet her and said, "Please give me a little water from your jar." ¹⁸"Drink, my lord," she said, and quickly lowered the jar to her hands and gave him a drink. ¹⁹After she had given him a drink, she said, "I'll draw water for your camels too, until they have finished drinking." ²⁰So she quickly emptied her jar into the trough, ran back to the well to draw more water, and drew enough for all his camels. ²¹Without saying a word, the man watched her closely to learn whether or not the Lord had made his journey successful. ²²When the camel had finished drinking, the man took out a gold nose ring weighing a beka and two gold bracelets weighing ten shekels. ²³Then he asked, "Whose daughter are you? Please tell me, is there room in your father's house for us to spend the night?" ²⁴And she said unto him, I am the daughter of Bethuel the son of Milcah, which she bare unto Nahor. ²⁵She said moreover unto him, we have both straw and provender enough, and room to lodge in. ²⁶Then the man bowed down and worshipped the Lord, saying, ²⁷"PRAISE BE TO THE LORD, THE GOD OF MY MASTER ABRAHAM, WHO HAS NOT ABANDONED HIS KINDNESS AND FAITHFULNESS TO MY MASTER. AS FOR ME, THE LORD HAS LED ME ON THE JOURNEY TO THE HOUSE OF MY MASTER'S RELATIVES"* (Genesis 24: 10-27; see also Proverbs 3: 5 – 6; 16: 1 – 3; Psalm 37: 3 - 5).

In view of these scripture, we can deduce that the Lord made Abraham's servant's journey to be successful because he committed his journey to God in prayer. He prayed for God to lead him and God led him to the house of his master's relatives according to the desires of Abraham. Without a doubt, God makes a believer's journey successful when it is committed to him in prayer, and that is why prayer is a walk with God. Prayer is asking God to lead while we follow. This explains the reason the Bible says,

> *"Trust in the LORD with all thine heart; and lean not unto thine own understanding. In all thy ways acknowledge him, and he shall direct thy paths" (Proverbs 3: 5-6, see also Psalm 37: 5).*

God led Abraham's servant to the well of waters at the right time when Rebecca, who was destined for Isaac, would be there. In the same manner, Solomon's prayer in the book of 2 Chronicles chapter 6: 17–21, and God's answer in chapter 7: 11–17 reveals a great deal and must re-kindle the fire of our prayer life if we are to be empowered for great and uncommon things.

It is evident in Paul's entire epistle that his encouragement to the brethren and his regular prayers for them insightfully helps to reveal that Paul was a man of prayer. Evidently, our Lord Jesus Christ is the epitome and perfect example when it comes to prayer. He lived a life of prayer on all occasion:

> *"And when he had sent the multitude away, HE WENT UP INTO A MOUNTAIN TO PRAY: AND WHEN THE EVENING WAS COME, HE WAS THERE ALONE" (Matthew 14: 23).*
>
> *"Then Jesus went with His disciples to a place called Gethsemane, and He said to them, "Sit here while I GO OVER THERE AND PRAY" (Matthew 26: 36).*
>
> *[39]"JESUS WENT OUT AS USUAL; AS WAS HIS HABIT TO THE MOUNT OF OLIVES, and His disciples followed Him. [40]On reaching the place, He said to them, "PRAY THAT YOU WILL NOT FALL INTO TEMPTATION." [41]HE WITHDREW ABOUT*

A STONE'S THROW FROM THEM AND KNELT DOWN AND PRAYED" (Luke 22: 39 – 41).

In His prayer on the eve of his crucifixion; Jesus prayed:

NEITHER PRAY I FOR THESE ALONE, BUT FOR THEM ALSO WHICH SHALL BELIEVE ON ME THROUGH THEIR WORD (John 17: 20).

Jesus prayed not only for his disciples, but *"also for all those who will believe in Him through our message."* If you will believe the spirit of the word ministering to your spirit from the pages of this book in faith to pray and see Jesus in that situation reversing the irreversible and moving your mountain, your life will know acceleration with every spiritual verity from God and cause you to excel so you can prosper in every area of your endeavours. This will grant you the knowledge and peace that you need to move all besieging mountain in your life.

Jesus' petition prayer in John 17: 23 was a request to the Father that believers might experience *"complete unity"* with one another and with God himself. Jesus asked the Father through prayer that we might enter fully into the fellowship that exists between himself and the Father. And that we might delight in his presence and behold his eternal glory. In this way the divine love of the Holy Trinity will be in us, and we in him (John 17: 26).

Indeed, true leadership is a product of inspiration as exemplified by Jesus who lived and taught what he preached. Jesus the epitome of prayer knowing the importance of prayer inspired his disciples to pray so they won't fall into temptation. Surely, there is power in prayer!

Jesus in his exemplary exegesis and manner, prayed for his disciples and also for everyone who will believe in him through their message. Jesus' petition with the father reveals his heart; that all believers might experience complete unity with one another and with God.

> "*15I pray not that thou shouldest take them out of the world, but that thou shouldest keep them from the evil. 16They are not of the world, even as I am not of the world. 17Sanctify them through thy truth: thy word is truth. 18As thou hast sent me into the world, even so have I also sent them into the world. 19And for their sakes I sanctify myself, that they also might be sanctified through the truth. 20Neither pray I for these alone, but for them also which shall believe on me through their word;21That they all may be one; as thou, Father, art in me, and I in thee, that they also may be one in us: that the world may believe that thou hast sent me. 22And the glory which thou gavest me I have given them; that they may be one, even as we are one: 23I in them, and thou in me, that they may be made perfect in one; and that the world may know that thou hast sent me, and hast loved them, as thou hast loved me. 24Father, I will that they also, whom thou hast given me, be with me where I am; that they may behold my glory, which thou hast given me: for thou lovedst me before the foundation of the world (John 17: 15-24).*

Jesus prayed to the Father on our behalf because he wants us to be an integral part of the communion that exists between himself and the Father, and for us to delight and behold his glory, being with him where he is. No wonder his disciples having observed his prayer life closely in Luke 11: 1 could ask him to teach them how to pray.

> *"And it came to pass, that, as he was praying in a certain place, when he ceased, one of his disciples said unto him, Lord, teach us to pray..." (Luke 11: 1).*

Taking a cue from all these, we can surmise that Jesus' inspiration is the divine deposit of destiny that must exist in the heart of every person of prayer. For instance, Peter who divinely observed the prayer life of Jesus and gained experience, knowledge and the understanding that is in the power of prayer admonishes us to be aware:

> "The end of all things is near. Therefore BE CLEAR-MINDED AND SELF-CONTROLLED SO THAT YOU CAN PRAY" (1 Peter 4: 7; see also 1 Peter 5: 8).

This lets us know that the believer needs to:

- *Be clear-minded so as to be focused and purposeful.*
- *Be self-controlled so you can be at peace with your inner-self able to pray effectively.*

These further tell us that for the believer to function and pray effectively, he must of necessity come to a place of resolve. This is because what you believe about yourself creates your world, and dictates your response to the present and determines the quality of your future. In other words, the quality of your vision determines your future. Therefore;

> *⁶Be careful for nothing; but in everything by prayer and supplication with thanksgiving let your requests be made known unto God. ⁷And the peace of God, which passes all understanding, shall keep your hearts and minds through Christ Jesus (Philippians 4: 6–7).*

If you neglect prayer, you neglect a divine destiny for your future. Don't neglect prayer; for it is the chisel you need to shape your tomorrow. Sincerely, there is power in prayer!

PRAYER EXERCISE

1. How is prayer a walk with God? See pages 119 - 121

_____

_____

_____

2. Give 2 scriptures that reveal Jesus
Christ as our epitome of prayer?

a. _____ *b.* _____

3. A walk with God is separation from: _____

(a) Friends (b) Family (c) The world (d) Work

4. How do you put the power of prayer into motion? See page 119 - 123

By ceaselessly praying and interceding for others.

5. Write 3 factors that helped to save Peter
from the hand of Herod in Acts 12?
See page 123 - 126.

_____

_____

_____

CHAPTER ELEVEN

HOW TO OPEN THE DOOR OF YOUR DESTINY WITH PRAYER?

*D*o you know you have a destiny in God? Are you aware many doors lead to your destiny? But not all doors are relevant to your destiny. This means you will have to discover and open the very door that leads to your destiny which you have been predestined to accomplish. *How do you open the door of your destiny?* The choice and decision of how you're to accomplish your destiny is within you and in your mouth. This is because God has ordained authority in your mouth for establishment, and has also made available to you the spirit of humility and all that pertain to life and godliness. Furthermore, the foremost thing you need to discover and accomplish your destiny is the power of prayer. This is what you need to open the door of your destiny! Secondly, you need to seek spiritual wisdom for insight that will help you make precise and right decisions at the hour of need through the power of prayer.

God has his deposits in you known as spiritual gifts, one of which is godly wisdom. This kind of wisdom is given to you from above so you can appropriate decisions. The very essence for which God endows with spiritual gifts is not just to perfect the saints but also for the saint to revolutionise his world and bring about godly change. As you continually confess the word and apply them to your life, they will begin to take root in you and manifest in reality. He says his authority is in your mouth and divine health is yours; sound mind is yours, strength is yours; prosperity and greatness belong to you because he has blessed you. He has blessed you indeed to affect your world with all these blessings which is why it matters how you live your life because you're God's representative on earth. With these it becomes imperative to have knowledge and understanding of the very door you must open to fulfil your destiny in God.

Literally speaking, to open a locked door is dependent on what key you have in your hand. This is the reason I'm letting you know that the door which leads to your destiny as a child of God is the name of the Lord Jesus, and the key that will open the right door which is the true way to your success and destiny is the power of prayer. This is the exact reason Jesus declared:

> "I am the WAY, the truth, and the life: no man cometh unto the Father, but by me" (John 14: 6).

The psalmist concurs and correlates saying,

> "The Lord is my shepherd...he leads me in the path of righteousness for his name's sake..." (Psalm 23: 1 & 3; read the entire psalm).

These let us know there are many reason the Lord leads the believer because:

- *The Lord is the way shower and Shepherd [protector] of the believer.*
- *It is for the Lord's name sake that he shepherds the believer and leads him to inherit eternal life.*

- *The believer who habitually dwells in his presence all of his days will be perpetually kept safe in the bosom of the Lord.*
- *Where the Lord leads, it becomes very easy to navigate your way to your destiny.*

These understanding of who the Lord is to the believer will help you to know how to open the door of your destiny with prayer. This is by appropriating an intimacy with the Lord because it is only through a humble, surrendered, submissive and teachable life that you can discover how your intimacy with the Lord can open the door of your destiny. However, it's expedient to know that there are many doors to a destiny as there are many keys to a door, but you need a specific key that will fit into the very door you want to open in order to define your purpose and walk in your destiny. This can only be accomplished when the Lord leads; for the Lord is the Shepherd of his people. He knows how to lead you through the wilderness of life, provide you with water from the rock and manna from above. He is the One that makes way where there seems to be no way and causes you to be strong and strengthened in your inner-man to estrange sickness, infirmity and diseases from your life. And because he is 'Grace', he will always keep you in perfect peace and make all your enemies to be at peace with you as he grants you favour before them to prosper abundantly (Isaiah 26: 3; Proverbs 16: 7).

Pertinently, it is imperative to know and understand that this particular door can only be opened through the key of the power of prayer made in the name of the Lord Jesus Christ. This is because the name of Jesus is the only name recognised in heaven and on earth for the door of your destiny to be opened (Philippians 2: 5 – 11). This reveals that the determinant to your surrendered, submissive intimate life with God is humility that's enabled to gain its life source by the power of prayer in the name of Jesus. In other words, the power of prayer is accomplished by the name of God's living word who is Jesus Christ. This further reveals that when you pray in the name of Jesus, the source of the power of prayer is the spirit of the **w**ord garnished by God's Holy Spirit. Evidently, the name of Jesus is the only most important key that you need as access to open the door of your destiny when you pray. This happens when you believe in Jesus with all your heart and have unfeigned faith in the word of God. This is because with faith we can please God when we stand resolutely on his word believing that he hears and wants all our needs met. This is why James could say,

> *"14 Is any sick among you? Let him call for the elders of the church; and let them pray over him, anointing him with oil IN THE NAME OF THE LORD [JESUS]: 15 And THE PRAYER OF FAITH SHALL SAVE the sick..." (James 5: 14-15).*

Here James emphasised that it is the prayer of faith that heals the sick in the name of the Lord Jesus. James understands the power of prayer; he knows and agrees that Prayer is the key in the hand of faith that opens the door of destiny. All of these expose for you to possess that which belongs to you in Christ Jesus you need to believe in yourself, you need to have faith in God and in the power of prayer. You must believe that whenever you pray God hears and will answer you. With this understanding, it becomes paramount and evident that you must always pray in the name of Jesus for your expected change to come regardless of your situation. This is because praying in the name of Jesus is the only way to your answered prayer as a believer. This is the right way to pray and explains the reason Jesus instructs us to pray in his name:

> *"Ye have not chosen me, but I have chosen you, and ordained you, that ye should go and bring forth fruit, and that your fruit should remain: that WHATSOEVER YE*

SHALL ASK OF THE FATHER IN MY NAME, HE MAY GIVE IT YOU" (John 15: 16).

"²³...I tell you the truth, my Father will give you whatever you ask in my name. ²⁴Until now you have not asked for anything in my name. Ask and you will receive, and your joy will be complete" (John 16: 23 - 24).

"13And I will do whatever you ask in my name, so that the Son may bring glory to the Father. ¹⁴You may ask me for anything in my name and I will do it" (John 14: 13 - 14 N.I.V).

This is one of the necessary means wherein we can bring forth fruit and see it abide because when we ask in the name of Jesus, God provides and meets all our needs causing the work of our hand to be established. In other words, the name of Jesus will open the door of your destiny! This is why the efficacy of the power of prayer made in the name of the Lord Jesus is the ability to produce the desired result.

When you look into the future of your destiny and it seems bleak and darkness looms, this is when to take Paul's admonition that says *"Pray in the spirit in all occasion with all kinds of prayer and supplication" (Ephesians 6: 18)* and pray without reservation until God's light shines through and prevails bringing transformation to your spirit, soul and body. When you understand the place of praying without ceasing and the authority vested in you in Christ Jesus, then will you be able to comprehend why the Bible talks about Shadrack, Meshach, and Abednego;

- *How they overcame the fiery furnace in the book of Daniel chapter 3: 8–30, and*
- *How Daniel also prayed and God shut up the mouth of lions when he was thrown into the lion's den in Daniel chapter 6: 1–23.*

Beloveth, have you ever been in a situation where you have been praying and praying, and praying the right way and nothing seems to happen? At such moment it looks as though you are standing alone; and seems as if fear wants to overwhelm you; this is the exact time to *believe* God's word the more and keep on praying for a change until something happens. Dispel fear and never allow fear into your spirit, it will disrupt your focus and conquer your belief; making your faith inoperative. Just believe and have faith that God hears and is doing something about your situation, and keep on praying and praying; don't lose focus but keep on thanking him until your expectations manifest and become a reality. Always Know, it is only *when:*

> *"The skies are full of rain that they empty themselves upon the earth" (Ecclesiastes 11: 3).*

The truth is that God cares and wants your needs met, and will meet them if only you will patiently persevere some more in prayer. This is because he rewards those who diligently seek him. This also means following him regardless of challenges and delays, not just for what you will get but because of who he is; knowing that his word is:

- *Infallible: [unfailing, certain, sure and absolutely reliable] (John 6: 63).*
- *Immutable: [unchanging, unalterable] (Luke 21: 33).*
- *Indestructible: [cannot be destroyed] (Hebrews 4: 12).*
- *Incorruptible: [pure, impossible to pervert, unsusceptible to decay] (1 Peter 1: 23), and*
- *Eternal: [everlasting, without end] (Psalm 12: 6; see also Genesis 15: 1-16).*

Obviously, anyone who desires an intimate relationship with God must of necessity be a man of persevering prayer; a never giving up fellow who's able to do. This makes tremendous power available to him. The Bible bears witness of Elijah as such a man:

> "*¹⁷Elias was a man subject to like passions as we are and he prayed earnestly that it might not rain: and it rained not on the earth by the space of three years and six months. ¹⁸And he prayed again, and the heaven gave rain, and the earth brought forth her fruit*" *(James 5: 17-18).*

Let your resolve always be to pray earnestly; Elijah prayed earnestly and God heard and brought his desires to fruition because Elijah as God's representative understood himself to be a man of authority whose word will not return void. This is the exact reason your resolve to pray earnestly, is so important if tremendous power is to be made available unto you. At this point having confidence in your prayer and knowing you are born of the Spirit of God will help you to decree a thing and see it established. This is so because your confidence in God helps to watch the intents of your heart by ensuring what and where you are directing your words to. You must not forget that every word you speak is a seed that is bound to reproduce itself because of the Spirit of God that is at work in you. This is why the Bible says,

> "*Verily I say unto you, whatsoever ye shall bind on earth shall be bound in heaven: and whatsoever ye shall loose on earth shall be loosed in heaven*" *(Matthew 18: 18).*

> "*Be not deceived; God is not mocked: for whatsoever a man soweth, that shall he also reap*" *(Galatians 6: 7).*

This is telling you to be careful of what you say with your mouth; be careful how you do what you do, be careful for nothing because every word you speak will reproduce it-self. Again, as a man of authority, always let those who encounter you praise

CHUCKS UZONWANNE

God for the gracious words that flows from your lips to your hearer's heart. Always let those who hear you be edified, and let them hear you gladly, giving glory to God. When you sow seeds of blessing into the life of others and witness the love of God to people, you are making tremendous power available and creating an atmosphere for miracles to take place as you pray for them. This is the kind of prayer God answers, when you live for his glory and become his vessel of blessing to others by helping them to discover their salvation in Christ Jesus. Look at it, the Bible speaks of Jesus saying,

> *"How God anointed Jesus of Nazareth with the Holy Ghost and with power: who went about doing good, and healing all that were oppressed of the devil; for God was with him" (Acts 10: 38).*

Can you now see who you are in the scripture I'm showing to you? Can you see yourself fitting into the picture frame of the word of God? This is what I'm showing you of who you are. Because Jesus is anointed; you are anointed. This is because you're born of his word and his Spirit; and his Holy Spirit is at work in you to will and to do of his good pleasure. You have been endued with the Holy Ghost and with power to function without limit. You now have your root in him because he is the vine and you are his branch; and have become his extension; for in him you live and move and have your being (see John 15: 1 & Acts 17: 28).

Do what Jesus is doing so you can get the kind of result Jesus is getting. The bible says that *"he went about doing good, and healing all that were oppressed of the devil; for God was with him."* Now it is glaringly revealed why Jesus was a man of prayer, so he can go about freely doing good and healing all the oppressed of the devil because the power of God was at work in him. So, go ahead and emulate Jesus in prayer and be empowered to move mountains and change hopeless situations.

Pray and lay your anointed hand in faith on the sick and see them recover and healed. Pray so that the power of God through you will bring salvation to sinners, and for them to experience the healing hand of God making the captives free and destroying yokes in the lives of those who are oppressed of the devil.

Whenever you pray for yourself, don't forsake praying for others; pray for the widows and the orphans. Pray for the innocent people locked up in the prison of men, and those in the dungeons under the clutches of darkness, and pray for those in hospitals all over the world. Don't stop now, keep on praying; pray for leaders of nations that they may receive salvation and know the Lord Jesus for them-selves. Pray for the grace of God to rest upon the servants of the Most High God to always speak the truth and judge rightly. Also, that they may receive grace in times of need and find favour with men to preach the gospel of our Lord Jesus without fear. Oh, don't stop now! Pray for your family, your siblings and your neighbours. Pray for your wife and for your husband. Pray for the bereaved woman whose husband just passed away. Pray for the lost son, lost daughter and the grieving family. Can you now feel the fire of the power of prayer rising, and fresh fire welling up within you to keep on praying. This is the exact reason you're holding the book in your hand and hearing what you're hearing in your spirit. Release that giant on the inside of you, so you can experience the tremendous power of prayer. This is awesome; just keep on soaking your spirit in prayer and keep on praying and pray more and more! Are you now saturated with prayer or you want some more? Has it gained ascendancy in your spirit? Go for more, always go for more; speak in tongues and don't stop now. Keep fuelling your prayer until it gains residency in you!

Go ahead and start over again with different prayer needs and keep on praying; pray until something happens. Break the yoke of ancestral covenanted spirits linked to you and destroy every works of darkness in your life, your family, your business, your relationship with men. Break the yoke of barrenness because you're born to be productive, the yoke of sickness for you're the healed of the Lord, the yoke of poverty and lack that the Lord Jesus exchanged for your riches. Break the yoke of frustration and disappointments and let the grace of God gain entrance and shine forth the light of the glory of God into your life. Pray for your life depends on it; and as you keep on praying see that mountain of problems removed and watch sickness disappear from your life. Just keep your gaze and focus on Jesus the author and finisher; the perfecter of your faith as you pray and see your husband, your wife, your brother, sister, son or daughter saved from the devices of the enemy. See them receive salvation and become saved. See you also receiving the gifts of the spirit, and believe that you or your wife have received the fruit of the womb and are pregnant with a male or female child. Call forth your desire this minute and see it manifesting in faith in the mighty name of Jesus Christ.

Add to your list and see you getting that desired Job; see that business blossoming in the name of Jesus Christ. Still in the attitude of prayer begin to see every ancestral hold, poverty and lack break free from you in the name of Jesus Christ. Whatever your desire, now that you have stirred the water of the spirit for the miraculous, go ahead and pray as you have the power to change that hopeless situation. Pray for peace in your life, in your marriage, in your family, your home and your place of work. Pray for the power of the favour of God to rest upon the works of your hand, upon your business, your family and to have favour with men because you have favour with God. Pray like you have never prayed before for this one thing and see it manifest in your life as the name of Jesus opens the door of your destiny! All glory to God.

CHAPTER TWELVE

YOU ARE AS IMPORTANT TO GOD AS YOUR PRAYER

The Bible records in the book of Revelation 5:8,

> *"⁸And when he had taken the book, the four beasts and twenty-four elders fell down before the Lamb, having every one of them harps, and GOLDEN VIALS [BOWLS] FULL OF ODOURS, WHICH ARE THE PRAYERS OF SAINTS."*

> *"³And another angel came and stood at the altar, having a golden censer; and there was given unto him much incense, that he should offer it with THE PRAYERS OF ALL SAINTS upon the golden altar which was before the throne. ⁴ And THE SMOKE OF THE INCENSE, WHICH CAME WITH THE PRAYERS OF THE SAINTS, ASCENDED UP BEFORE GOD OUT OF THE ANGEL'S HAND" (Revelation 8: 3-4).*

These scriptures reveal how important your prayers are to God. It shows you are as important and valued to God as your prayers. Your prayers are so very important to God to the intent angels in heaven are waiting for you to pray so they can present your prayers as incense before God. This is because God has placed a high premium value on you as an intercessor. So much so, your prayers move the hand of God to determine consequences on earth.

"*20...And the LORD said, Because the cry of Sodom and Gomorrah is great, and because their sin is very grievous; 21I will go down now, and see whether they have done altogether according to the cry of it, which is come unto me; and if not, I will know. 22And the men turned their faces from thence, and went toward Sodom: but Abraham stood yet before the LORD. 23And Abraham drew near, and said, Wilt thou also destroy the righteous with the wicked? 24Peradventure there be fifty righteous within the city: wilt thou also destroy and not spare the place for the fifty righteous that are therein? 25That be far from thee to do after this manner, to slay the righteous with the wicked: and that the righteous should be as the wicked, that be far from thee: Shall not the Judge of all the earth do right? 26And the LORD said, If I find in Sodom fifty righteous within the city, then I will spare the entire place for their sakes. 27And Abraham answered and said, Behold now, I have taken upon me to speak unto the Lord, which am but dust and ashes: 28Peradventure there shall lack five of the fifty righteous: wilt thou destroy all the city for lack of five? And he said, if I find there forty and five, I will not destroy it. 29And he spake unto him yet again, and said, Peradventure there shall be forty found there. And he said, I will not do it for forty's sake. 30And he said unto him, Oh let not the Lord be angry, and I will speak: Peradventure there shall thirty be found there. And he said, I will not do it, if I find thirty there. 31And he said, Behold now, I have taken upon me to speak unto the Lord: Peradventure there shall be twenty found there. And he said, I will not destroy it for twenty's sake. ³²And he said, Oh let not the Lord be angry, and I will speak yet but this once: Peradventure ten shall be found there. And he said, I will not destroy it for ten's sake. ³³And the LORD went his way, as soon as he had left communing with Abraham..." (Genesis 18: 20-33).*

This is the very reason I encourage every believing person to always pray and intercede for others because God expects you to stand in the gap for them. Understand this, if you were not significant to God, neither will your prayers be important to him. You must understand that he chose and separated you unto himself for works of righteousness. He equipped you to go and bring forth fruit; this means he prices you above all creation and expects you to produce both spiritual and physical fruits that will abound and make a difference in the lives of men for his name's sake (John 15).

You're so preciously valued that God says you are the apple of his eye and will not leave you until he has fulfilled his purposes for your destiny so your life can reflect his glory. That is why he is in you and with you to will and to do of his good pleasure. This means he's doing good and blessing men everywhere through you because of your intercessory prayers. This is the very reason you must not relent in your prayers because whenever you pray either for you or intercede for others, God is in you and with you approving of your good works. This is because through you he is healing the oppressed and redeeming his people. So settle it that you are not alone whether in times of trouble or in the time of safety.

You must not misunderstand who you are with what you're going through because you're a genuine and bona-fide child of God, born of his Spirit. That situation is the trial of your faith; and like a mirage it will soon fade away if you persist in prayer. This is because you are a victor in Christ Jesus; the very reason you're more than a conqueror and an overcomer because the greater One

CHUCKS UZONWANNE

dwells in you (1 John 4: 4). Having this understanding that even now where you are this minute, God's eyes are on you and his ears are attentive to hear your prayers if you will go on your knees and pray in faith. This will work wonders in your life if you will confess God's right words over that situation and observe everything turn around for your good. This is because the scriptures reveal that the prayers of the saints come before God as incense and further reveals that God will use your prayers to chart the course of life and make you walk in your destiny.

Another way of seeing it, is that your prayers determine whether evil prevail in the earth or not, with blood sucking demons causing accidents, and wrecking havoc in the lives of men. Whether disasters such as hurricane, floods, volcanic eruptions, whirlwind, avalanche, drought, landslides, tornado and the likes can be changed or stopped, and whether sickness, infirmities and diseases are healed depends largely on your intercessory prayers and those of other saints. This is how important you and your prayers are to God.

> *"And it shall come to pass, that before they call, I will answer; and while they are yet speaking, I will hear"*
> *(Isaiah 65: 24; see also Deuteronomy 10: 12 - 13).*

No wonder those that walked with God in the Bible days never over emphasised the place of the power of prayer. They believed so much in prayer that they became the people of prayer! Here, I'm talking about the likes of *Abraham, Moses, Joshua, Elijah, Elisha, Jacob, Esther, Nehemiah, Daniel, Isaiah* and many other great prophets of God who performed incredible fits. All of these were people who prayed having understood the power of prayer and made a difference in the history of mankind because God was with them.

Apparently, we are the saints of our time, and if we desire to walk with God and produce the kind of results they produced in the Bible days; then we must of necessity pray like they prayed and do the things that made them formidable. This means that by learning to pray, we must pray and keep on praying until we receive answers to our prayers. Obviously, a relationship with God makes our Prayer life excitingly efficacious especially when it becomes regular habit practiced in the right way. The story of Cornelius in Acts 10 and how God sent his angel to encourage him to receive salvation in the name of Jesus through Peter's preaching and all those who were present gives another insight on how we are to apply the power of prayer and let the light of Christ shine in the recesses of our community to open the door of destiny and usher in salvation for all repentant hearts when we intercede prayerfully. It is only righteousness that exalts a nation and this delights God to see the work of salvation effectively carried to the latter as people everywhere lift up holy hands and give their hearts to him. This means that his injunction to *"Go into the entire world and preach the gospel"* must be strictly adhered to without compromise because this is the power of God unto salvation to everyone who believes (see Proverbs 13: 34; 1 Timothy 2: 8; Romans 1: 16).

> *"¹At Caesarea there was a man named Cornelius, a centurion in what was known as the Italian regiment. ²HE AND ALL HIS FAMILY WERE DEVOUT AND GOD-FEARING; HE GAVE GENEROUSLY TO THOSE IN NEED AND PRAYED TO GOD REGULARLY. ³One day at about three in the afternoon he had a vision. He distinctly saw an angel of God, who came to him and said, "Cornelius!" ⁴Cornelius stared at him in fear. "What is it, Lord?" he asked. The angel answered, "YOUR PRAYERS AND GIFTS TO THE POOR HAVE COME UP AS A MEMORIAL OFFERING BEFORE GOD..." (Acts 10: 1 – 4).*

CHUCKS UZONWANNE

The previewed scripture reveals Cornelius as devout and a great man of prayer whose contrasting image speaks volume. This fierce and extremely powerful man of war feared God and prayed regularly to God with his family and gave generously to the needy. These verses depict how remarkable the character of Cornelius was, and distinguished him amongst his peers:

- *A centurion of the Italian regiment, and yet feared God with his family.*
- *He was trained to be a tough and uncompromising leader, and yet very tender in heart.*
- *He was respected and loved by those around him because of his love for humanity and love for God.*
- *He was powerful and yet approachable because of his submissiveness to God.*
- *He was a no-nonsense leader, yet a loving father and caring friend who gave arms generously.*

Certainly, we can see how Cornelius's contrasting image of strength and humility opened the door of his destiny through the power of prayer and positioned him with God. This battle-hardened leader of the world's toughest soldiers was a humble man who prayed with his family regularly. He was a giver of alms whose charitable donation to the poor and needy precedes his reputation, even before God.

This positive influence of ceaseless devotion to God and humanity can help the present day believer to be strong and humble; submissive and devoted to God. It will encourage every praying saint to better understand how he is to establish an intimacy with God through the power of prayer.

Evidently, Cornelius modelled for all believers the need to not only be humble and submissive to God, but also to stand in the gap and ensure that family, friends, our community and our nation at large regularly spend quality time with God by expressing the selfless God kind of love to them.

The truth is, most times when believers pray, some are ignorant and oblivious of the impact their prayers make in the realms of the spirit. This makes them relent and treat the things of God with levity because they don't think much is being achieved. This is because they're looking with their optical eyes and seeing only the earth realm. Another reason they're spiritually not mature enough to look with the eyes of faith and to see into the realms of the spirit is because they're impaired, and so, cannot see the importance and impact of their prayers. This means they lack faith in the word of God, and don't believe they have the inherent ability in themselves to effect a change because of lack of intimacy with the Lord. Furthermore, they're short sighted and blinded by their feelings; therefore they don't believe God values their prayers enough to change their circumstances.

For these reasons many that have problems which demands them praying to effect a positive change, faint and would not pray. They want to be reminded and cajoled to pray thinking they're doing someone big favours if they prayed by themselves. And for some, the only time they pray is when they're in trouble; and that is when you see them in Church hovering over the pastor.

Some others even confess that they can't pray, so they're looking for someone to pray on their behalf, as though the person they'll get to pray on their behalf has the solution to their problems. Whatever your circumstance, you must learn to pray for yourself and never rely on some other person because God wants to hear you pray specifically. He knows you can pray because his ability is in you. All you need do is to come out of your comfort zone and pray, fast, and wait on him in faith.

Always pray believing! Never pray in unbelief! Never doubt yourself and never, ever quit praying! Believe in the word of God, and believe that God hears and is willing to answer and meet your needs as you pray. To under estimate yourself is to undermine your capability in God and make God less who he is. You must never under any circumstance belittle the power of prayer because you have been empowered to decree a thing for it to be established. Always remember there is power in the word you speak and that's what makes you valued and very important to God. Another thing is to always pray with the word because every word rightly applied from God through you are right seeds that will reproduce once they're sown. It therefore matters what you sow and the ground to which you sow. If you must reap a good harvest then go ahead and sow good seeds, praying with the word in the name of Jesus. Sow good seeds through prayer; scatter them upon the waters and watch your life and those around you bear bountiful harvest. All glory to God!

CHAPTER THIRTEEN

THE NECESSITY OF PRAYER

"Pray without ceasing" (1 Thessalonians 5: 17).

"...to this end, men ought always to pray and not to faint..." (Luke 18: 1).

What is your opinion on prayer? Do you think prayer is a waste of time? Should you always pray or not? Do you think prayer is a basic necessity in your life as a believer? If your opinion is contrary to the above scriptures and you're implying that prayer is an expensive waste of time, therefore not necessary, then wait and see the bill that ignorance will serve you. Because you have chosen not to pray, ignorance will serve you with the bill of:

- *Ungodliness, tale bearing, telling of lies, wickedness.*
- *Unbelief, disobedience, foolish pride, jealousy.*
- *Unrighteousness, hatred, sickness, infirmity, diseases.*
- *Spiritual blindness, fear of the unknown, unfocused life amongst other vices.*

Due to some people's act of moral corruption and depravity, these many live in the city of ungodliness and complacency;

feeling cool, thinking and saying to themselves, *"relax men, we're in control of our life and nothing can happen. Don't mind those preachers and church goers who carry Bible and talk about God all the time. Go ahead and smoke and drink all sorts; become a booze addict and tell lies. Live recklessly in unrighteousness and don't worry about anything; God understands." You don't need their preaching to make heaven, and you definitely don't need their preaching to survive tomorrow. If you survived today on booze you will definitely survive tomorrow..."* and so they live on survival lane singing *"what will be will be"* They knowing full well; the only thing that will be is poverty and hangover, pain, sorrow, suffering, sickness, infirmity, disease, lack, death, and hell that they created for themselves. Some even make themselves government property and choose to be called the degenerates of society. These are unperturbed and unsusceptible to change at the expense and peril of their future.

What makes you think if you don't do something about your life now the way you are going that you will be able to do something about your life tomorrow? Today is the opportunity you have to receive Jesus Christ into your life and be fulfilled. Do you think the opportunity you have now will be waiting perpetually for you? You need to know that what you tolerate today, you cannot change tomorrow. This means only you can change you to become who you desire yourself to be! Invariably, it is how and what you think you are that you'll become. There is a saying that *'those who show up go up; and for you to go up, you need to grow up.'* Make a wise decision this minute to receive Jesus Christ into your heart as your Lord and Saviour especially now it concerns you and your future.

In martial arts you will learn that the best form of defence is attack. Attack or you will be attacked. This implies that you don't give room to ignorance; so attack unrighteousness, ungodliness and complacency with prayer and the word of God before your inadequacies bring you down.

After giving your heart to Christ; always pray for revelation knowledge, do something worthwhile and productive to occupy your time with, and this will enable you attack:

- *poverty, pain, suffering*
- *sickness, disease, infirmity, lack*
- *And you'll see all unwanted situations give way.*

Also remember that this revealed knowledge comes as a result of the word of God, and faith is necessary when you pray to believe and to act on the word and all contrary conditions.

> *"[21]Jesus answered and said unto them, Verily I say unto you, If ye have faith, and doubt not, ye shall not only do this which is done to the fig tree, but also if ye shall say unto this mountain, Be thou removed, and be thou cast into the sea; it shall be done. [22]AND ALL THINGS, WHATSOEVER YE SHALL ASK IN PRAYER, BELIEVING, YE SHALL RECEIVE" (Matthew 21: 21-22).*

The story of this parable told by Jesus is very remarkable. It reveals that the hand that pray is the heart that receives because it trusts in the Lord. Every believer must pray always to avoid ignorance. This will help to keep their focus right in perspective. The believer must learn to have faith in God so he can be abreast of situations and able to remove mountains when he prays, and positively change the lives of those in his sphere of contact and the society at large.

Why is prayer necessary? Prayer is necessary because it helps you maintain fellowship with God and gives you sound mind. It helps you gain spiritual insight and direction, and motivates you to be at peace with all men. Prayer helps you to walk in victory over ungodliness and to have dominion over anything and everything both seen and unseen that are contrary to the word of God. We

CHUCKS UZONWANNE

must not wait until there is trouble before we can pray because *prayer serves as the guiding hand that brings to us the blessings which God has already provided.*

Apparently, with the knowledge of the word of God and prayer, change becomes inevitable and certain. And so it becomes imperative that the understanding the believer has of the word, prayer and faith will put him at an advantage to overcome in times of adversity because he carries the personality of the word of God on the inside of him. This also indicates that he is born of God because God's Spirit is at work in him. This is what makes him an over-comer because the greater one now lives in him.

> *"Ye are of God, little children, and have overcome them: because greater is he that is in you, than he that is in the world" (1 John 4: 4).*

> *"For whatsoever is born of God overcometh the world: and this is the victory that overcometh the world, even our faith" (1 John 5: 4).*

Do not wait until there is trouble before you can pray; start now to pray even if you don't have a need for one yet. Get yourself ready and always be prepared to pray. This is one of the reasons the Bible informs of the necessity of prayer and encourages you to pray at all times. This arms you with the knowledge and understanding that *prayer is the opening of the heart to God as to a friend (see 1 Thessalonians 5: 17-18).*

Because God loves you, he comes to you in moments when you open your heart to him through the power of prayer. This means that whenever you pray, your confidence is built in God and your faith increases because it is solidly laid on the right foundation. So go ahead and pray always for it is a good solid foundation.

When you familiarise yourself with prayer, it will help to alley your fears, position you for dominion and bring you fulfilment as it charts the course of your life. For these reasons the necessity for prayer cannot be over emphasized. There is power in prayer that can change any hopeless situation, and help to define and give meaning to your life if you will regularly pray. For instance, with prayer the believer can have peace even in time of trouble and be confident that God is with him because he is standing on God's promises in faith.

> *15And when the servant of the man of God was risen early, and gone forth, behold, an host compassed the city both with horses and chariots. And his servant said unto him, alas, my master! How shall we do? 16And he answered, Fear not: for they that be with us are more than they that be with them. 17AND ELISHA PRAYED, AND SAID, LORD, I PRAY THEE, OPEN HIS EYES, THAT HE MAY SEE. AND THE LORD OPENED THE EYES OF THE YOUNG MAN; AND HE SAW: and, behold, the mountain was full of horses and chariots of fire round about Elisha. 18AND WHEN THEY CAME DOWN TO HIM, ELISHA PRAYED UNTO THE LORD, AND SAID, SMITE THIS PEOPLE, I PRAY THEE, WITH BLINDNESS. AND HE SMOTE THEM WITH BLINDNESS ACCORDING TO THE WORD OF ELISHA (2 Kings 6: 15-18).*

This makes prayer an excitable and intimate relationship which by grace invites the believer to present his case before the living God. *Did you notice that God smote the Syrians with blindness at the request of Elisha?* This is very insightful and powerful because it reveals that the praying believer has authority in his tongue and the assurance that whenever he prays he can unlock heaven's storehouse and gain access into the boundless resources of Omnipotence.

"Death and life are in the power of the tongue: and they that love it shall eat the fruit thereof" (Proverbs 18: 21).

This is so because God wishes for his children to take charge of situations, therefore equips their tongue with authority to speak, be protected and for their needs to be met. Here was humanly speaking an unbelievable scenario; Elisha was in trouble with the King of Syria who summoned soldiers to capture him. On getting to Elisha's place one would suppose that Elisha would either have fled before they got to him or beg them as they come, instead Elisha was unperturbed and at peace even at their presence because of whom he has believed whose he is. *Why was Elisha so relaxed and at peace?* As a praying man, his confidence was in the intimate relationship he has established with God through the power of prayer which was evident in his words:

- *Firstly, Elisha prayed for the eyes of his servant to be opened for him to see the protection his confidence was made of. And at that instance, the Lord opened the eyes of his servant to see innumerable company of angels surrounding Elisha and as his servant saw them he maintained his peace.*
- *Secondly, one can discern the power of prayer in action when Elisha prayed for God to cover all the Syrian army with blindness and immediately the Lord obliged him with his request. The irony was that those that came to capture Elisha became his captives.*
- *And thirdly, when Elisha commanded the blind Syrian army to follow him to Samaria; on getting to Samaria he also prayed to the Lord to open their blind eyes and the Lord obliged him his prayer request and opened the eyes of the Syrian army.*

Isn't it great and wonderful to know there is power in prayer? This power in prayer is in your tongue and will put you at a vantage point if you will speak forth to proclaim the word of God with power in the name of Jesus. It will position you to be focused and to see beyond your immediate circumstance which was the case with Elisha.

He saw beyond the immediate and took advantage of what the situation provided and turned it around for good. There is no gainsaying that God's supernatural grace was with Elisha and working mightily in his favour. This is because no ordinary human being can make the human eyes to see into the realms of the spirit or go blind, and at the same time get the blind eyes opened again. If we were talking about an individual someone would probably try to reason it out, but for a whole army of soldiers to go blind at the request of an individual has to be the mighty hand of God at work in his anointed one because of his devoted prayer life. Another case scenario is the remarkable man of God by name Daniel. Listen to what he has to say:

> *9...Yet heard I the voice of his words: and when I heard the voice of his words, then was I in a deep sleep on my face, and my face toward the ground. 10And, behold, a hand touched me, which set me upon my knees and upon the palms of my hands. 11And he said unto me, O Daniel, a man greatly beloved, understand the words that I speak unto thee, and stand upright: for unto thee am I now sent. And when he had spoken these words unto me, I stood trembling. 12THEN SAID HE UNTO ME, FEAR NOT, DANIEL: FOR FROM THE FIRST DAY THAT THOU DIDST SET THINE HEART TO UNDERSTAND AND TO CHASTEN THYSELF BEFORE THY GOD, THY WORDS WERE HEARD, AND I AM COME FOR THY WORDS. 13But the prince of the kingdom of Persia withstood me one and twenty*

CHUCKS UZONWANNE

days: but, lo, Michael, one of the chief princes, came to help
me; and I remained there with the kings of Persia. [14]Now
I am come to make thee understand what shall befall thy
people in the latter days: for yet the vision is for many days
(Daniel 10: 9 - 14).

This revelation further stresses why every believer must always pray and not relent. It unveils the power of prayer, in that, whether or not someone receives depends on his ability to persevere and keep on praying until his prayer is heard. It exposes and also invites an intimacy of steadfastness that guarantees genuine reverence for God with the understanding that he is our source and therefore sufficient for us. If Daniel had stopped praying after a few days, he wouldn't have been envisioned to know what the future held in stock for him and his people, neither would he have been able to receive the revelation from the angel of what was happening around him in the realms of the spirit.

Take note of what the angel said; it was the words of Daniel in prayer and his preparation to understand what God held in stock for his people that informed the perseverance of the angel even though he was withstood by the prince of Persia for 3 weeks.

[12]Then said he unto me, Fear not, Daniel: for from
the first day that thou didst set thine heart to understand,
and to chasten thyself before thy God, thy words were
heard, and I am come for thy words. [13]But the prince of
the kingdom of Persia withstood me one and twenty days...
(Daniel 10: 12-13).

Having looked at some of the scriptures, one can conclude that it is imperative to pray always without which little or nothing can be achieved. Yes! It is expedient that every believer must pray because prayer is the key in the hand of faith that opens the door of destiny. Do not forget that a prayer-less mind is a troubled soul.

That prayer changes everything and helps to restore peace in times of need [trouble] proves positive the necessity for prayer.

At creation, God's plan was to create a world of beauty where human beings would be able to procreate, and nature produce at the request of man. All in the light of man worshipping God and having a relationship with him. But somewhere along the line man disobeyed and things fell apart; nature was distorted and the relationship that once existed between God and man was lost. It became apparent that man needed a means to rekindle the lost bond and this lost bond was re-established through the power of prayer because men began to call on God (Genesis 4: 26). So, prayer became an important medium wherein man relates with his maker because prayer is spiritual. Praying to God shows how merciful God is and reveals his grace; his willingness to pardon and meet every need. God desires for his children to be happy; fulfilled and lack nothing. He wants to meet all your needs this instant. This is why when you pray, asking in expectation, positions you to receive because you're acting in faith.

7Ask and it shall be given you; Seek, and you shall find; knock and it shall be opened unto you: 8For everyone that asketh receiveth; and he that seeketh findeth; and to him that knocketh it shall be opened (Matthew 7: 7 – 8).

Do you know that if it were not possible to pray to God, God wouldn't have encouraged us to pray to him? This is why when you ask, it means you're praying, when you seek, you're praying and when you knock, you're also praying because at this point your expectation is to receive the object of your desire. It is because God knows how beneficial it is for us to ask in prayer that compels him to go the extra mile to bless us. When you pray, as long as your desire is in consonance with God's word, your heart desires will become yours for the asking if you believe it and act in faith. And for your prayer to be heard and answered, you will need to believe in the One to whom you are praying; that he is able to change your circumstances and meet your needs according to his word that says,

> "...But my God shall supply all your need according to his riches in glory by Christ Jesus...." (Philippians 4: 19 see also 1 John 5: 14-15).

For this to be yours at this point, you will need to do something worthwhile by positioning yourself to be where God wants you to be. Be where he can reach you and bless you. For instance, Jesus said to his disciples in Acts 1: 4-5:

> ⁴And, being assembled together with them, commanded them that they should not depart from Jerusalem, but wait for the promise of the Father, which, saith he, ye have heard of me. ⁵For John truly baptized with water; but ye shall be baptized with the Holy Ghost not many days hence.

If you read the book of Acts starting from chapter one to four, you will discover that the disciples of Jesus had to remain in Jerusalem where Jesus required for them to be in order for the Holy Spirit to come upon them.

Imagine if the disciples of Jesus hadn't remained in Jerusalem prayerfully obeying the instructions given to them by Jesus. The Holy Spirit would have come to Jerusalem where they were expected to be, and they would have missed their empowerment and not have been able to accomplish great fits recorded in the book of Acts of the Apostles. Don't forget, it was after the Holy Spirit had infused them, that they were energized with boldness and faith to preach and perform beyond human imaginations. For instance, Peter and John were on their way to the temple at the hour of prayer.

See the beautiful account in Acts chapter 3 and conclude for yourself if what transpired would have been able to take place if they hadn't been praying and endued with the Holy Spirit:

¹Now Peter and John went up together into the temple at the hour of prayer, being the ninth hour. ²And a certain man lame from his mother's womb was carried, whom they laid daily at the gate of the temple which is called Beautiful, to ask alms of them that entered into the temple; ³Who seeing Peter and John about to go into the temple asked an alms. ⁴And Peter, fastening his eyes upon him with John, said, Look on us. ⁵And HE GAVE HEED UNTO THEM, EXPECTING TO RECEIVE SOMETHING OF THEM. ⁶THEN PETER SAID, SILVER AND GOLD HAVE I NONE; BUT SUCH AS I HAVE GIVE I THEE: IN THE NAME OF JESUS CHRIST OF NAZARETH RISE UP AND WALK. ⁷And he took him by the right hand, and lifted him up: and immediately his feet and ankle bones received strength. ⁸And he leaping up stood, and walked, and entered with them into the temple, walking, and leaping, and praising God. ⁹And all the people saw him walking and praising God: ¹⁰And they knew that it was he which sat for alms at the Beautiful gate of the temple: and they were filled with wonder and amazement at that which had happened unto him. ¹¹And as the lame man which was healed held Peter and John, all the people ran together unto them in the porch that is called Solomon's, greatly wondering. ¹²And when Peter saw it, he answered unto the people, ye men of Israel, why marvel ye at this? Or why look ye so earnestly on us, as though by our own power or holiness we had made this man to walk? ¹³The God of Abraham, and of Isaac, and of Jacob, the God of our fathers, hath glorified his Son Jesus...¹⁶AND HIS NAME THROUGH FAITH IN HIS

CHUCKS UZONWANNE

NAME HATH MADE THIS MAN STRONG, WHOM YE SEE AND KNOW: YEA, THE FAITH WHICH IS BY HIM HATH GIVEN HIM THIS PERFECT SOUNDNESS IN THE PRESENCE OF YOU ALL. (Acts 3: 1-16).

Notice the boldness of Peter and John who but for the endowment of the Holy Spirit wouldn't have dared come out in public for fear of the Pharisees. But after that the Holy Spirit had come upon them, the spirit of boldness and utterance was given to them to function effectively and miracles became a common place with them. This you can deduce as you read the scriptures below, of how Peter and John were addressing the people, the priests, captain of the temple and the Sadducees came to the scene and were grieved that they taught the people and preached in the name of Jesus, the resurrection from the dead. The amazing thing was that five thousand men believed the gospel of Peter and John and gave their hearts to Jesus in one ministration, glory to God. Also notice that they were put in prison and interrogated by the highest authority of their day, and with boldness Peter filled with the Holy Spirit ministered to them undermining their threats.

> *¹And as they spake unto the people, the priests, and the captain of the temple, and the Sadducees, came upon them, ²Being grieved that they taught the people, and preached through Jesus the resurrection from the dead. ³And they laid hands on them, and put them in hold unto the next day: for it was now eventide. ⁴Howbeit many of them which heard the word believed; and the number of the men was about five thousand.*

> *⁵And it came to pass on the morrow, that their rulers, and elders, and scribes, ⁶And Annas the high priest, and Caiaphas, and John, and Alexander, and as many as were*

of the kindred of the high priest, were gathered together at Jerusalem. ⁷And when they had set them in the midst, they asked, by what power, or by what name, have ye done this? ⁸*THEN PETER, FILLED WITH THE HOLY GHOST, SAID UNTO THEM, Ye rulers of the people, and elders of Israel,* ⁹*If we this day be examined of the good deed done to the impotent man, by what means he is made whole;* ¹⁰*Be it known unto you all, and to all the people of Israel, that by the name of Jesus Christ of Nazareth, whom ye crucified, whom God raised from the dead, even by him doth this man stand here before you whole.* ¹¹*This is the stone which was set at nought of you builders, which is become the head of the corner.* ¹²*Neither is there salvation in any other: for there is none other name under heaven given among men, whereby we must be saved.* ¹³*NOW WHEN THEY SAW THE BOLDNESS OF PETER AND JOHN, AND PERCEIVED THAT THEY WERE UNLEARNED AND IGNORANT MEN, THEY MARVELLED; AND THEY TOOK KNOWLEDGE OF THEM, THAT THEY HAD BEEN WITH JESUS.* ¹⁴*And beholding the man which was healed standing with them, they could say nothing against it.* ¹⁵*But when they had commanded them to go aside out of the council, they conferred among themselves,* ¹⁶*SAYING, WHAT SHALL WE DO TO THESE MEN? FOR THAT INDEED A NOTABLE MIRACLE HATH BEEN DONE BY THEM IS MANIFEST TO ALL THEM THAT DWELL IN JERUSALEM; AND WE CANNOT DENY IT.* ¹⁷*But that it spread no further among the people let us straitly threaten them that they speak henceforth to no man in this name.* ¹⁸*And they called them, and commanded them not to speak at all nor teach in the name of Jesus.* ¹⁹*BUT PETER AND JOHN ANSWERED AND SAID UNTO THEM, WHETHER IT BE RIGHT IN THE SIGHT*

CHUCKS UZONWANNE

OF GOD TO HEARKEN UNTO YOU MORE THAN UNTO GOD, JUDGE YE. [20]FOR WE CANNOT BUT SPEAK THE THINGS WHICH WE HAVE SEEN AND HEARD (Acts 4: 1 - 20).

The question now is, *are you where God wants you to be?* If you are, and you are sure of it then don't worry about a thing, for God will surely answer you in his right time. This is because he makes all things beautiful in his time. But, if you are not where you are supposed to be, and you certainly know you are not, this is the time to relocate yourself and move up to where God wants you to be and position yourself for your greatness is about to emerge.

The disciples were where they were instructed to be, and at the appointed time, the Holy Spirit came upon every one of them and they began to do great and wondrous things. So I urge and encourage you not to be weary in praying, just keep on

"Casting your bread upon the waters, for after many days you will surely find it" (Ecclesiastes 11: 1).

Do not cast off restraint, do not fret, nor forget that, it is only *"when the skies are full of rain, that they empty themselves upon the earth" (Ecclesiastes 11: 3 see also 1 Kings 18: 41-45).* Let your prayer saturate heaven like in the case of Daniel, Cornelius, Elisha and Elijah. There has to be the gathering of the clouds first, for the emptying to take place, and it takes some time for that to happen. This means that your turn will come, just keep at what you believe God for, and keep fuelling it with the power of prayer, and the doors of destiny shall be opened unto you sooner than you can imagine.

"Now unto him that is able to do exceeding abundantly above all that we ask or think, according to the power that worketh in us" (Ephesians 3: 20).

If you observe closely you will notice that because the disciples where at the right place and at the right time many advantages can be seen in the above scripture that accrued to them.

Notice that regardless of the intimidation of the priests, captain of the temple and the Sadducees it did not deter Peter and John to preach there, of which about five thousand men believed and were saved.

- *Reason being that timidity left them at the point of their empowerment. It is only when the Holy Spirit is upon a man that transformation takes place and turns him into another being with boldness to accomplish supernatural fits. This means that Peter and John were infused and transfigured by the Holy Spirit to get besides themselves and do uncommon things beyond human comprehension.*
- *Secondly, when they were brought out of the prison the next day and began interrogating Peter and John, the Bible said that Peter was filled with the Holy Spirit and began to proclaim to all the leaders, scribes and as many as were of the house of the high priest that the miracle that took place was in the name of Jesus. This reveals that there is something about the name of Jesus that excites your confidence and makes you bold beyond the ordinary.*
- *Thirdly, when they saw the boldness of Peter and John, they perceived that they were unlearned and ignorant men and marvelled because they took knowledge of them that they had been with Jesus. Like I said, before the spirit of boldness and the supernatural will come upon you, the Holy Spirit has to take over and be in control of you. This will make people notice you differently that you are a true disciple of Jesus and a child of God just like they spoke of Peter and John testifying that they had been with Jesus. This is also because God is able to do through you exceeding, abundantly above all that you*

may ask or think according to his mighty power that is at work in you (Ephesians 3: 20).

- *Fourthly, seeing the man which was healed standing with them, the Bible records that they could say nothing against Peter and John other than to threaten them and that didn't deter the disciples one bit. So do not fret or be anxious about anything. Rather;*

> *"⁶Be careful for nothing; but in everything by prayer and supplication with thanksgiving let your requests be made known unto God. ⁷And the peace of God, which passeth all understanding, shall keep your hearts and minds through Christ Jesus" (Philippians 4: 6-7).*

When a believer asks God for something in the name of Jesus, God provides him with the opportunity to receive that which he has asked for by positioning him with favour to receive that which he is acting on his believe for. And for him to receive it, he must see it with the eyes of faith and be thankful to God for it. Sometimes, it is difficult to know what to pray for and how to pray when faced with adverse situations. This is when you need the Holy Spirit the most. You need to realise there are different kinds of prayers; so, you need to know what kind of prayer to apply in a giving circumstance. Knowledge of what to do and how to pray will put you over when adversity shows up because you are prepared and know what to do. Such knowledge comes through the discovery of an intimate relationship with the one to whom you are praying. When you make being in his presence a part of you; that is, you've learnt to spend quality time with him in his presence; you will begin to have revelation knowledge and the experiences of deep spiritual insights will be unveiled to you. This is because you're being led by the Spirit of God on what to do in every given situation.

"Praying always with all prayer and supplication in the Spirit, and watching thereunto with all perseverance and supplication for all saints" (Ephesians 6:18).

This scripture encourages every believer to pray regularly with different kinds of prayer and to especially make requests in the spirit and patiently wait on the Lord perseveringly, which means, you can pray in the language of your understanding as well as speak in tongues, but also you must be patient to receive answers to your prayer. Sometimes when you don't know what to pray about, your only option will be to speak in tongues, that way, the Holy Spirit will come to your aid in prayer and before you know it, you are refreshed and full of words again, to intercede for others as you pray for yourself.

"[26]Likewise the Spirit also helpeth our infirmities: for we know not what we should pray for as we ought: but the Spirit itself [himself] maketh intercession for us with groanings which cannot be uttered. [27]And he that searcheth the hearts knoweth what is the mind of the Spirit, because he maketh intercession for the saints according to the will of God" (Romans 8: 26-27).

CHUCKS UZONWANNE

PRAYER EXERCISE

1. Why is prayer necessary? See page 154 - 157

_____

_____

_____

2. Write 3 bills ignorance will serve you
   if you don't pray? See page 154

_____

_____

_____

3. What are the 2 things you need to avoid
   ignorance? See page 154 - 156

_____

_____

4. Which of these scriptures reveals the three
   ways of praying? See page 162 - 163

   (a) Matthew 7: 7 – 8 (b) 1 Thessalonians
   5: 17 (c) Philippians 4: 6

5. Name 3 abilities the Holy Spirit gives when
   He comes upon a man? See page 163 - 170

_____

_____

_____

CHAPTER FOURTEEN

CAN GOD MEET MY NEEDS WITHOUT MY PRAYING

"But my God shall supply all your need according to his riches in glory by Christ Jesus" (Philippians 4: 19).

When I was a young boy growing up, I grew up knowing the do's and the don'ts in our home. I remember my father had his rules and likewise my mother. The rule in our home engaged me with certain level of responsibilities. They were for my adherence and benefit in that it helped me to be in my parent's good books. This also afforded me access to certain things that ordinarily I couldn't have had access to. For example, I learnt to drive at the age of twelve by merely watching my dad and elder brother drive. Whenever my dad returned from work and parked his car that is when I would offer to wash the car for him. That way, I tried my hands on some of the things I learnt secretly during my outing with him. And that went on extensively for days, weeks and over a given period of time. My dad had noticed that the car was not always the way he parked it each time I took the keys to wash the car, and so he thought to find out how. He knew my elder brother was hardly at home; if he's not at school then he was always either on tour with the Lagos state handball team or at the stadium or Row Park where he's engaged in training with the Lagos state hand ball team. Besides, my brother would ask for the car keys if he wanted to drive the car. And so, on this faithful day, oblivious that my dad was standing behind me while I was fiddling with the steering; he caught me in the very act when I started the car and moved it.

My point is, in every family there are rules! In like manner, God has set rules for those in his kingdom. These set rules are laid down principles that define his do's and don'ts; they govern his kingdom both in heaven and on earth for the benefit of all. For instance, the laws of God help every believer in the family of God to receive salvation and to walk in righteousness and holiness, to discover their destiny and be fulfilled.

As a member of the family of God, you ought to understand the rules of the family unless of course if you are a baby or an outsider. What am I saying, no outsider can be found in the kingdom because there are no strangers in the family of God. Let's face it that you are a baby is understandable but not an excuse. Even as a baby you still need to follow the rules. That means your adherence to the rules will benefit you because they will mature you and help you gain knowledge and understanding of who you are and what is expected of you. So, as a baby you will be feeding on milk alright and won't have need for strong meat until you come to maturity. But it does not excuse your obedience to the rules of the family.

This just means that you will need someone to guide and help you to stand on your feet; someone who can encourage you to walk and speak the language of the kingdom, and also help you to study the word; teaching you what is what in the kingdom and how to pray the right way. This is why even as a baby, you're still subject to the rules of the kingdom because of the one guiding you.

Don't you think, It will be unimaginable if your six months old baby begins to talk and make a demand for your car keys or if he begins to make a demand for cigarette and booze. Every reasonable parent will not oblige their babies anything that would harm or put them in harm's way. So such requests will be a definite no! Invariably, the question of whether God would meet my needs if I don't pray depends on what those needs are and your level of maturity. The direct answer to the question is a definite no! This is because God needs your prayer to judge consequences. If your request is something you can get on your own, then you don't need God to get them. This can only mean one thing; that you may struggle to get them since you want to get them by your own power and not through the grace of God. If you're a baby, there is a level to which you can ask for something and it will be given to you because the one who gives it to you knows it's in adherence or consonance with the word of the rules of the kingdom. On the other hand, a full grown man will have to obey the rules before his request can be granted. Understandably, God wants to meet all our needs according to the previewed scripture, but he will not violate his rules just so you can prove a point. If you knowingly refuse to adhere to the rules how do you think God will for your sakes bend his own rules. This means for your needs to be met, you will have to get those needs met on your own because you have refused to obey the word of God. This brings to remembrance the story of the disciples of Jesus who left their calling and went back to their circular fishing business, and they began to struggle because that was not what God intended for them. They struggled and kept on struggling until the Lord Jesus came on the scene and restored them. It is only when the Lord Jesus steps into the boat of your life that the course of your life can be navigated to your destiny. Another inference of a great prophet that struggled the minute he chose to lose focus as a result of disobedience is Jonah. He so lost it that his life was in jeopardy until he repented and grace rescued and restored him. Hear what the Bible has to say:

> "*¹Now the word of the LORD came unto Jonah the son of Amittai, saying, ²Arise, go to Nineveh, that great city, and cry against it; for their wickedness is come up*

before me. [3]But Jonah rose up to flee unto Tarshish from the presence of the LORD, and went down to Joppa; and he found a ship going to Tarshish: so he paid the fare thereof, and went down into it, to go with them unto Tarshish from the presence of the LORD. [4]But the LORD sent out a great wind into the sea, and there was a mighty tempest in the sea, so that the ship was like to be broken. [5]Then the mariners were afraid, and cried every man unto his god, and cast forth the wares that was in the ship into the sea, to lighten it of them. But Jonah was gone down into the sides of the ship; and he lay, and was fast asleep. [6]So the shipmaster came to him and said unto him; what meanest thou, O sleeper? Arise, call upon thy God, if so be that God will think upon us, that we perish not. [7]And they said everyone to his fellow, Come, and let us cast lots, that we may know for whose cause this evil is upon us. So they cast lots, and the lot fell upon Jonah. [8]Then said they unto him, Tell us, we pray thee, for whose cause this evil is upon us; what is thine occupation? And whence comest thou? What is thy country? And of what people art thou? [9]And he said unto them, I am a Hebrew; and I fear the LORD, the God of heaven, which hath made the sea and the dry land.

[10]Then were the men exceedingly afraid, and said unto him, why hast thou done this? For the men knew that he fled from the presence of the LORD, because he had told them. [11]Then said they unto him, what shall we do unto thee, that the sea may be calm unto us? For the sea wrought, and was tempestuous. [12]And he said unto them, Take me up, and cast me forth into the sea; so shall the sea be calm unto you: for I know that for my sake this great tempest is upon you. [13]Nevertheless the men rowed hard to bring it to the land; but they could not: for the sea wrought, and was tempestuous against them. [14]Wherefore they cried unto the LORD, and said, we beseech thee, O LORD, we beseech

thee, let us not perish for this man's life, and lay not upon us innocent blood: for thou, O LORD, hast done as it pleased thee. ^{15} So they took up Jonah, and cast him forth into the sea: and the sea ceased from her raging. ^{16} Then the men feared the LORD exceedingly, and offered a sacrifice unto the LORD, and made vows. ^{17} Now the LORD had prepared a great fish to swallow up Jonah. And Jonah was in the belly of the fish three days and three nights" (John 1: 1-17).

"^{1} Then Jonah prayed unto the LORD his God out of the fish's belly, ^{2} And said, I cried by reason of mine affliction unto the LORD, and he heard me; out of the belly of hell cried I, and thou heardest my voice. ^{3} For thou hadst cast me into the deep, in the midst of the seas; and the floods compassed me about: all thy billows and thy waves passed over me. ^{4} Then I said, I am cast out of thy sight; yet I will look again toward thy holy temple. ^{5} The waters compassed me about, even to the soul: the depth closed me round about; the weeds were wrapped about my head. ^{6} I went down to the bottoms of the mountains; the earth with her bars was about me forever: yet hast thou brought up my life from corruption, O LORD my God. ^{7} When my soul fainted within me I remembered the LORD: and my prayer came in unto thee, into thine holy temple. ^{8} They that observe lying vanities forsake their own mercy. ^{9} But I will sacrifice unto thee with the voice of thanksgiving; I will pay that that I have vowed. Salvation is of the LORD. ^{10} And the LORD spake unto the fish, and it vomited out Jonah upon the dry land" (Jonah 2: 1-10).

As a child of God, your struggling will end today if you will discover and obey and do God's will for your life. Don't follow status – quo, only follow God through Jesus Christ and the Holy Spirit will lead you to fulfil God's purpose for your life. Observe that Jonah was given an assignment to go to Nineveh, but he chose to ignore it and went on a personal cruise to Tarshish. On his way when trouble brewed as a result of his disobedience the mighty tempest enraged the sea and Jonah knew for what intent the seas were troubled. Take note that it was the Lord that sent the great wind; in as much as Jonah thought he could escape from the presence of the Lord. And the mariners knew this was happening because someone in their midst was responsible for the evil that befell them... 7And they said everyone to his fellow, Come, and let us cast lots, that we may know for whose cause this evil is upon us. So they cast lots, and the lot fell upon Jonah. 8Then said they unto him, Tell us, we pray thee, for whose cause this evil is upon us; what is thine occupation? And whence comest thou? What is thy country? And of what people art thou? 9And he said unto them, I am a Hebrew; and I fear the LORD, the God of heaven, which hath made the sea and the dry land. 10Then were the men exceedingly afraid, and said unto him, why hast thou done this? (Jonah 1: 7-10).

Many a time out of ignorance, the children of God do things of grave consequences and think they can get away with it. The down side is that it affects everyone within knowingly or unknowingly. This is why it is expedient to always pray because with prayer you will not only establish a firm relationship with God, but it will also help you to know the will of God for you, and also help others to recover themselves. I need you to realise that it was until Jonah repented and began to pray that the Lord commanded the great fish to vomit Jonah. Because Jonah knew in his circumstance that the only hope he had left was to pray. This is another reason why prayer is the key in the hand of faith that opens the door of destiny. This is the very essence which makes it dangerous to assume that if you don't pray that God will meet your need. If Jonah hadn't prayed when he did, most likely the hand of fate would have been reversed and he would have suffocated because God preserved him to teach him a lesson; and he learnt the hard way for the Bible says:

"*¹Then Jonah prayed unto the LORD his God out of the fish's belly, ²And said, I cried by reason of mine affliction unto the LORD, and he heard me; out of the belly of hell cried I, and thou heardest my voice...¹⁰And the LORD spake unto the fish, and it vomited out Jonah upon the dry land*" (Jonah 2: 1-2 &10).

You can deduce some important lesson from the experience of Jonah that made him to pray:

- *You must not wait until you're confined before you can pray.*
- *Don't wait until you suffer affliction before you can pray to God.*
- *Don't allow the ungodly system of this world to swallow you before you can pray.*
- *And don't live in the vomit of the system before you can pray*

It is until you look up to God for mercy in the moment of your affliction that the Lord will bring up your life from corruption, but your prayer must ascend up to him right into his holy temple like an incense. Otherwise you may forsake your own mercy because of the wrong thoughts driving your passion. Did you catch another revelation from Jonah's experience to know that running from the presence of the Lord is not an option; it will not only cost you but can also put everyone around you in danger? The Bible says,

¹³Nevertheless the men rowed hard to bring it to the land; but they could not: for the sea wrought, and was tempestuous against them. ¹⁴Wherefore they cried unto the LORD, and said, we beseech thee, O LORD, we beseech thee, let us not perish for this man's life, and lay not upon us innocent blood: for thou, O LORD, hast done as it pleased thee. ¹⁵So they took up Jonah, and cast him forth into the sea: and the sea ceased from her raging (Jonah 1: 13-15).

CHAPTER FIFTEEN

PRAYER, BELIEF AND FAITH

We having the same spirit of faith, according as it is written, I believed, and therefore have I spoken; we also believe, and therefore speak (2 Corinthians 4: 13).

It is very important first of all to understand what the above scripture is saying, this will help to clarify what faith is made up of and to understand it's source before we can talk about prayer and belief. The scripture we have just read gives an insight and explains that faith is a spirit. *'We have the same spirit of faith...'* It says. It is therefore important that we take note of this because it is the determinant to the rest of the discussion on faith. It also tells us the source of faith *'...according as it is written...'* This makes it clear that faith is from the word of God because it is written in the volume of the book of life. This also implies that nothing outside the word of God can inspire this kind of faith in a human person.

The beauty of it all is that you need to believe in your faith and declare it before it can work for you *'...I believed and therefore have I spoken; we also believe and therefore speak.'* This implies that for your faith to work for you it has to be activated by you acting on the concepts of your belief and expectation. *Isn't it wonderful to know that you have faith and must believe in it for it to work for you?*

Clarifying this further, we need to know there are factors that determine what motivates our prayer, faith and belief system. For one to effectively pray it becomes imperative to believe wholeheartedly that God and his word co-exists as one therefore requires that we believe in what the word says and act in faith for the word to take effect in our lives. This is the major determinant of these factors. Another determinant is because God is faith-God, it becomes impossible to please him without faith. You need to act in faith before him who calls forth things that be not as thou they already existed. So, for you to be able to effectively operate the values of prayer, belief and faith you need a standpoint.

Call it a vantage position from where you can clearly see these values and apply them in your life for results. Your vantage position is your ability to see into the realms of the spirit, and this becomes the determinant to *what you see, how you see, what you believe, how you pray, and how your faith would work.* Liken your standpoint to two words: *'Optimism' and 'pessimism.'* It's either you are an optimistic person or a pessimist; this means you're either positively or negatively dispositioned.

Now I need you to know that these are powerful forces that define your personal expectations of success or failure. They determine the effectiveness of your prayer life and faith and influence what happens to your belief system. These powerful forces to a large extent are crucial to your perceptivity and attitude to actions and reactions, your environment and life as a whole. The overview of these concept help to determine how you think, how you see things, challenges in life, the decisions you make and their outcome. This also determines whether you feel good or bad about yourself, and your perceptivity in turn affects your thought pattern and can directly influence how you feel from time to time. So, be an optimist and see life from the standpoint of God. A pessimist does not believe and cannot have this kind of faith no matter what. So, don't be a pessimist, it can only derail your thought pattern to be negative and this will incapacitate and keep you inactive!

In the face of opposition, chaos and confusion, the first step to dealing with such problems is to identify the root cause of the problem. Believe it is solvable and imperturbably keep your focus on the solution in faith. That is, be optimistic in your resolve and with prayer seek direction for a permanent solution. This goes to say that *'if you don't aspire to something, you won't have focus; if you don't have focus; you will never achieve purpose.'*

For you to achieve purpose therefore, you need to visualise it with the eyes of faith. *If you don't visualise it, you won't believe it nor can you activate your faith to accomplish it.* Therefore, to positively and effectively ideate a vision, you need the power of prayer. *Why vision?* It is so because your vision determines your future. Vision is very expedient for precedence in life because it is determined by our disposition, perception and paradigm. This indicates that a life without a vision will soon wither and die. With a vision, you can believe and prayerfully chart the course of your life.

For you to conceptualise it you need to visualise it in order to realise it. And this is made possible through the lens of faith because God is 'now' and he is exclusively relational. It becomes difficult and challenging to conceptualise something if you are not always positive. Your being positive will help your disposition to see things from a godly perspective. This is where the power of imagination gives birth to faith and your believe. It is a highly effective means of applying faith to accomplish vision. Reason that Helen Keller said, *'The worst thing that could happen to someone is to have sight without vision.'* And the Bible further intones that,

> *"Where there is no vision, the people cast off restraint..."(Proverbs 29: 18).*

Many are without vision and those who dared to visualise cannot conceptualise for lack of faith, stolen by fear of the unknown. They forget that all aspects of life are about perspective and visualisation which is a precursor *[announcer, precedent, antecedent, and predecessor]* that defines your faith and belief system. It is very important that you shape your future reality by your visuals of today. This means that *'the power of your future lies in the concepts of your 'now'.'* In other words, what you do with the present moment determines what your future will become. This also means that your *attitude determines your altitude.*

If you introspect and retrospect, you will discover that your life until this minute is what it is because of the choices and decisions you made in the past. Here you are today with another chance to have a firm grip of your life and this chance of a positive change is now! *What choices and decisions would you make if you desired a better tomorrow and a great future?* The choices and decisions you make this minute will determine what happens to your tomorrow. One thing you must not do is to be afraid to try and afraid to fail. You will have nothing to lose if you try and fail. If you fail and choose to arise, it becomes an added knowledge to you on how to get better when next you try because your experience for trying points you to the right direction for success. However, if you don't try, you will not fail because you already have failed; neither can you succeed until you try.

No wonder Albert Einstein said, *"It's not that I'm so smart, it's just that I stay with problems longer."*

Consequently, when you try and experience the turbulence of life and it seems you have failed, prayerfully stay with it and seek a solution on what next to do in that circumstance that will change the hopeless situation. This will open for you a myriad of opportunities and advantages if you will not relent but learn from it to gain knowledge that would position you for your tomorrow. The right way to do this is by cleaning the lens of your perception and sharpening your think-ability to look and see things from a faith dimension; that is, to have godly perspective and see with the vista of God. At this instance, it is expedient that you forget your past failures and look on the sunny side of life.

To look on the sunny side of life, however, you must quit eating the bread of sorrows and stop crying over spilt milk. This will only remind you of your past legacy of failures and keep you incapacitated because they will come at you with such intensity like a flood aiming to overthrow a city if you don't change your paradigm with the power of prayer and speak forth positive right words.

Do not pay attention to the legacies of your past failure; they will not help you where you are going now! As a matter of fact, you don't need them. Settle it in your heart that you don't need them. At this point, you must learn to be cautious by taking an inventory of your life and make it your responsibility to change your situation and to succeed by being optimistic and positively confessing the right words to the situation. Considering your vantage position now that you are beginning to see the advantage in your disadvantages, it stands to reason that you would have done some things differently if you facilitated and harnessed your new vantage position which now opens you up to better concepts on how to turn your past failures into a great success. Don't make it complex and more difficult for yourself, you need to look beyond the situation and work at achieving your purpose one step at a time keeping in mind the overview of your destiny. This is when to immovably stand on the word of God, believe in the vision of yourself and habitually pray. And be passionate about whatever you love to do that you have envisioned. This is that time that requires the reinforcement for you to irrefutably believe in the word of God and to exact your faith.

To prayerfully and unswervingly keep your perspective on the object of your meditation at this point, it becomes expedient that you place a value on these objects of your desire.

Why place a value on your desire considering the complexity of your situation? The value becomes the yard-stick for measuring the height of your ascension and this will help to mobilise your focus for your achievement. This is so because it stretches and gives you an aspiration that makes feeling valued one of the cornerstones of your sense of wellbeing and this will help to challenge and build your faith giving you the required confidence which is your needed inspiration to overcome your difficulties and be fulfilled. For example, every sportsman's expectation is to win a medal; the medal provides them with a focus to look forward to during competitions. This becomes the yard-stick for measuring their performance because of the value attached to the medal. It is like dangling a carrot before a horse to motivate his journey. The value you have placed will help to broaden your horizon for success and position you to attain and achieve it now that you believe you can regardless of the odds because of the resilient ability in you known as the *'will to do'* engineered by the power of prayer. This serves as a transporter for the motivation of your perspective to see and be strengthened in your inner-man. This is the possibility of your walking through an open door of greatness and success that defines achievement and the fulfilment of your destiny. You must not feel insignificant nor should you look with the tiring eye of disillusionment. Against all odds, you must see with the eyes of faith; this is because nothing shall be impossible unto him that believes.

Case Scenario

[17]And one of the multitude answered and said, Master, I have brought unto thee my son, which hath a dumb spirit; [18]And wheresoever he taketh him, he teareth him: and he foameth, and gnasheth with his teeth, and pineth away: and I spake to thy disciples that they should cast him out; and they could not. [19]He answereth him, and

CHUCKS UZONWANNE

saith, O faithless generation, how long shall I be with you? How long shall I suffer you? Bring him unto me. ²⁰And they brought him unto him: and when he saw him, straightway the spirit tare him; and he fell on the ground, and wallowed foaming. ²¹And he asked his father, how long is it ago since this came unto him? And he said, of a child. ²²And oft times it hath cast him into the fire, and into the waters, to destroy him: but if thou canst do anything, have compassion on us, and help us. ²³Jesus said unto him, If thou canst believe, all things are possible to him that believeth. ²⁴And straightway the father of the child cried out, and said with tears, Lord, I believe; help thou mine unbelief. ²⁵When Jesus saw that the people came running together, he rebuked the foul spirit, saying unto him, Thou dumb and deaf spirit, I charge thee, come out of him, and enter no more into him. ²⁶And the spirit cried, and rent him sore, and came out of him: and he was as one dead; insomuch that many said, He is dead. ²⁷But Jesus took him by the hand, and lifted him up; and he arose. ²⁸And when he was come into the house, his disciples asked him privately, why could not we cast him out? ²⁹And he said unto them, this kind can come forth by nothing, but by prayer and fasting (Mark 9: 14 – 29; see also Matthew 17: 14-21).

Here was a remarkable story of faith which would have been an opportunity for the disciples of Jesus to prove their mettle, but the interesting thing was that they couldn't in as much as they tried. Jesus made it clear why they couldn't; they lacked prayer and faith *'…and I spake to thy disciples that they should cast him out; and they could not. ¹⁹Jesus answereth him, and saith, O faithless generation..'* Their faith could not be activated in the first place because they did not believe they could. They tried but they couldn't because of their lack of prayer and fasting.

'...¹⁹When Jesus was come into the house, his disciples asked him privately, why could not we cast him out? ²¹And Jesus said unto them, this kind can come forth by nothing, but by prayer and fasting' (Mark 9: 28 – 29; see also Matthew 17: 19 – 21).*

Is your faith being inspired and are you motivated to pray this minute? This is the essence for the book in your hand. As you keep reading, the power of prayer will transport you to a higher realm and motivate you to do what it says. *Tell me with all these insightful revelation if you were at the scene with the disciples of Jesus would you have made a difference?* This is why you need to study more, pray more and exercise your faith always for results. Don't take no for an answer! *Do you know that however insignificant you may feel about yourself for failing, life is still a truly wonderful gift if only you can see the beauty of your effect on others? Are you asking 'how can this be'?* This is so because we are all linked to each other and affect the lives of one another in ways that are beyond our control. Therefore, as you drive that vehicle of apathy and self worthlessness, don't park your emotions on the pathway of melancholy looking for passengers to pay you with sorry and sympathy. In other words, as you go through the highways, byways and pathways of life the relevant thing that determines the success of your destination is the vehicle driving your thoughts, your paradigm and your perspective? Critical to it all is the feeling behind your thoughts; how you look becomes the determinant to what you see.

This is when you need to be positive about life the most; otherwise you might be swayed and derailed by wrong thoughts and forfeit a great destiny. This is the exact time when, if you say you can, you can because the choices you make now will define the decisions that will influence what your tomorrow and future

CHUCKS UZONWANNE

will become. Don't forget *'confidence comes not from always being right but from not fearing to be wrong.'*

Do you really want to change your situation? Are you prepared to accept that you'll need to do some things differently from now on? An honest answer to these questions could be the difference between where you are presently and where God has predestined for you to be.

This could make the difference between success and failure in your life, by you establishing a relationship through prayer that would put you over and above your challenges. At this instance you might be slightly unsure particularly when it definitely means you have to do some things differently. Of course, you will need to accept that seeking a solution might be difficult because it will entail you having to break some old habits. Change is the most difficult thing to adapt, yet it is constant more so if your life depends on it. If you weigh the risk of trying at the back drop of where you are now, the decision of whether you will succeed or fail is with you. Try to think of this as the proverbial journey of a 1,000 mile that starts with a step. Until you resolve to take the necessary right and first steps, you may remain in the rut that you have put yourself. So, you need to see your situation as a project that you must accomplish and place a value on, by so doing; you will be motivated to take the necessary risk for a positive change. As with all projects it will only succeed if it is thoroughly planned and effectively prepared for through the power of prayer and you believing for it in faith.

Factors that motivate success:

-   *Study, read and learn.*
-   *Meditate, assimilate and reflect.*
-   *Be specific about your challenges and need.*
-   *Believe the word as you apply the word to your challenges through prayer.*

- *Exercise your faith by acting on your believe.*
- *Trust that God heard your prayer and that your answer is on its way.*
- *Be completely resolute regardless of how you feel, what you see and what you hear that is opposed to the word of God.*
- *Stand firmly on the word and be expectant for the manifestation of your request.*
- *Be humble and teachable for grace to open the door of your destiny.*

Let's face it, why are you reading this book? Apparently, you may have a personal reason or there could be various reasons that motivate your reading this book of all books. That it appeals to you could either be that you are looking to establish an effective prayer life, a relationship with God or that you are in a hopeless situation seeking solutions. Whatever your reason, one thing is certain, the power of prayer will help you to establish an intimate relationship with God and also help you to develop a hunger for study and prayer that will help you to believe and exact your faith. The power of prayer will guide and teach you on what to do to come out of seeming difficulties that are beyond you when you adhere to the truth.

Some people are faced with problems they ignorantly allowed to accumulate in their lives to the extent that they don't know how to go about solving it anymore.

These are challenges which they can't overcome because they lack the discipline to study, pray and relate intimately with the one who has the solution to all life problems - Almighty God.

Others are struggling with all sorts of spiritual issues relating to prayer, faith and belief; and ignorantly don't know what to do even when they're so close to solutions, but the fear of the unknown keeps them away from reality. Or perhaps you are one of the people who don't have major issues requiring prayer. You need to bear in mind that as you embark on your journey in life, you will discover that several roads are linked. Some to life and some others to destruction, but the one that leads to life is usually rocky yet good. This means those that lead to destruction are smooth roads with no curves and bumps that look alright at the onset but are bad and impenetrable road that reveals itself as you keep travelling. While the rocky are good roads with curves, bumps, and pot holes that need only to be addressed at the onset after which the journey is smooth sailing. For these reasons only a few find it because not many are willing to patiently attempt.

> *¹³Enter ye in at the strait gate: FOR WIDE IS THE GATE, AND BROAD IS THE WAY, THAT LEADETH TO DESTRUCTION, AND MANY THERE BE WHICH GO IN THERE AT: ¹⁴Because STRAIT IS THE GATE, AND NARROW IS THE WAY, WHICH LEADETH UNTO LIFE, AND FEW THERE BE THAT FIND IT (Matthew 7: 13-14).*

You will have to decide for yourself which road to take and the consequences for each encounter you experience. This is when you would realise that it's not just seeking a quick fix solution that you need to make a difference because a quick fix is temporary, but seeking for the right and permanent solution that is golden and lasting will effect the needed change. And this can only be achieved by effective prayer that is cultivated through intimate relationship with the One who is the way, the truth and the life. For you, I believe this is where the power of prayer will become resourceful, in that, it will become your compass to accompany you discover the right road that will engender your prayer life and help you find fellowship with the one who is able to do exceeding abundantly above all that you may ask or think, who answers to all prayer. Don't forget all these can only be achieved through the power of prayer.

CHAPTER SIXTEEN

WHAT IS PRAYER?

However insignificant or fulfilled in life one may feel, someone somewhere is thinking on how to change hopeless situations, exchange thoughts and ideas, talk intimately with someone for solutions, intercede on behalf of friends and siblings, and desires communication with his maker. This implies that by faith, prayer is the concept of your perceived thoughts presented to God that prompts the receipt of your expected desire based on your belief in the word and relationship with God. In other words, *prayer is an exchange of thought that helps you commune intimately with God for solutions on issues beyond your control.* This is because *prayer is a cultivated relationship based on believed concepts of principles between the applicator and the promises [the word] of the one able to effect a change.* Obviously and without exception, *prayer is a petition or application to God expressed in words or thoughts.* This further explains why *prayer is the unveiling of the heart to God based on his word. This is responsible for the reason the bible says:*

> "And whatsoever we ask, we receive of him, because we keep his commandments, and do those things that are pleasing in his sight" (1 John 3: 22).

If I may ask, *is there anyone who does not have the desire to pray even if they don't know how?* Everyone at some point I presume wants to pray, because people everywhere have needs and want their problems solved. This is because they believe God answers prayers and can solve their problems. So they want an answer to all the questions that conditions and circumstances create. These and many other reason makes it obvious and imperative for people to want to pray, which is why the Bible enjoins us to:

> *"Pray without ceasing" (1 Thessalonians 5: 17; see also*
> *1 Timothy 2: 1-4, 8).*

Sometimes people don't know they are praying by the things they say and do because of the level of their ability to perceive. However, it is not so much that people pray that is in question here but, when you pray; *are your prayers in consonance with the knowledge of the word of God? Are you praying in line with God's perfect will for your desire? Do you really know to whom you're praying?* Are you praying the right way?

You need to understand that prayer is a life-long relationship that is cultivated for the hand of God to rest upon the believer. It is not so much for meeting needs only but also for you to understand God's perfect will concerning others on what to do to make the world a better place. In other words, when you understand the perfect will of God for your life half your problem is solved because this creates an awareness that positions you to walk in the light of spiritual verities. Imagine a scenario where believers all over the world with the understanding of the place of prayer are praying and fasting for leaders of nations, communities and people; the world will be a safer place for all. Thank God many have imbibed this practice:

> *"²¹Then I proclaimed a fast there, at the river of Ahava*
> *that we might afflict ourselves before our God, to seek of*

him a right way for us, and for our little ones, and for all
our substance. ²²For I was ashamed to require of the king a
band of soldiers and horsemen to help us against the enemy
in the way: because we had spoken unto the king, saying,
The hand of our God is upon all them for good that seek
him; but his power and his wrath is against all them that
forsake him. ²³So we fasted and besought our God for this:
and he was intreated of us (Ezra 8: 21-23).

This scripture is talking about danger in the face of opposition. Of how Ezra and his people returned to Jerusalem because the hand of the Lord his God was upon them. Convinced that God was with them, Ezra proclaimed a fast and prayer for all the people, and did not ask king Artaxerxes for soldiers to protect them against their enemies on the way even though the king was willing to grant them soldiers knowing that danger awaits them. Rather, Ezra trusted in the Lord his God because he made it clear to the king that the hand of God was upon them for protection, and the Lord heard their prayer.

Prayer will give you an insight to comprehend the thoughts of God concerning you and those around you, and this will make you ask according to the basic principles based on the word of God. This is because you now have knowledge and know what you should be asking for. At this level, you're asking with accurate knowledge and in consonance with the perfect will of God for you.

"¹I exhort therefore, that, first of all, supplications,
prayers, intercessions, and giving of thanks, be made for
all men; ²For kings, and for all that are in authority; that
we may lead a quiet and peaceable life in all godliness and
honesty. ³For this is good and acceptable in the sight of God
our Saviour; ⁴Who will have all men to be saved and to
come unto the knowledge of the truth" (1Timothy 2: 1-4).

CHUCKS UZONWANNE

The scripture we've just read reveals that prayer is to be made for all men including kings and those in authority that we may live a quiet and peaceable life in all godliness and honesty. This is because it is good and acceptable in the sight of God. He went further to reveal how this can be possible; when all men are saved and come to the knowledge of the truth. This inaugurates that *prayer must be intimately selfless, overwhelmingly transforming and result oriented.* It concurs that *prayer brings you to the place of spiritual awareness that positions you for insight into reality and makes you want to do the essentially important.*

This actually explains why the disciples of Jesus asked Jesus to teach them how to pray. *Why would the disciples of Jesus ask to be taught how to pray? Is it that they have not been praying before their encounter with Jesus or that they discovered uniqueness in Jesus' prayer life?* All of these question points to one conclusion and that is that Jesus consistently communed with the Father in a way that is unique and different from what they were used to. His communion with the Father was so effectively strong and result oriented that by his spoken word and a touch he raised the dead to life, and opened blind eyes; deaf ears were opened and the lame walked. These and many mighty works [miracles] performed by our Lord Jesus Christ explains some of the reasons his disciples could not resist asking him to teach them how to pray so they can be as effective in prayer by learning the right way to pray. Let's listen to their conversation and gain more insight:

> *¹And it came to pass, that, as he was praying in a certain place, when he ceased, one of his disciples said unto him, Lord, teach us to pray, as John also taught his disciples. ²And he said unto them, when ye pray, say, Our Father which art in heaven, Hallowed be thy name. Thy kingdom come. Thy will be done, as in heaven, so in earth. ³Give us day by day our daily bread.*

⁴And forgive us our sins; for we also forgive every one that is indebted to us. And lead us not into temptation; but deliver us from evil (Luke 11: 1-4; see also Matthew 6: 5 - 13).

Jesus led a model prayer life and his disciples knew it. The Bible says:

"...as he was praying in a certain place, when he ceased, one of his disciples said unto him, Lord, teach us to pray..."(Luke 11: 1).

For Jesus' disciples to have been that convinced to ask him to teach them how to pray means they have been observing Jesus pray a long time, perhaps before they met with him. These Jews were so convinced of his prayer life that they desired for him to teach them how to obtain similar results.

In this brief *'model prayer'* taught by Jesus to his disciples, the Lord Jesus gives an outline that may be used for all prayers which is why this teaching when observed very closely is a guide that would help the believer to know:

- how to come into the presence of God
- how to present his request
- And what to expect in return.

The details of this prayer pattern demonstrate:

- reverence for God
- an assertive belief in his purposes for his children
- And dependence on his provision.

Whenever you stand before God in prayer, purpose demand that whatever your area of need; revelation knowledge is what is required to actualise those needs. Revelation knowledge is insight into the reality of what you need as opposed to your wants based on God's word. This means that in your moments of need don't just accept anything and everything that the situation throws at you. Filter your need with the word and take those that are urgently relevant to your circumstance, and attend to them with utmost care prayerfully. Be specific and precise when you stand before God with your petitions, that way, you'll know the purpose and promises of God for you.

> "Pray that the Lord your God may show [you] the way
> in which [you] should walk and the thing that [you] should
> do" (Jeremiah 42: 3 Amp) Emphasis mine.

To ensure that what you are praying about is indeed what you need, revelation knowledge or insight into reality is crucial to your resolve, that way; you remain unshakeable and immoveable because you predicate your confidence on the word of God. This is the understanding of the revealed spiritual verities that defines the things you are asking from God which will in turn establish your faith and strengthen your believe to receive. The Bible further clarifies this in the praying words of Apostle Paul thus:

> [17] That the God of our Lord Jesus Christ, the Father of
> glory, may give unto you the spirit of wisdom and revelation
> in the knowledge of him: [18] The eyes of your understanding
> being enlightened; that ye may know what is the hope of his
> calling, and what the riches of the glory of his inheritance
> in the saints, [19] And what is the exceeding greatness of his
> power to us-ward who believe, according to the working of
> his mighty power (Ephesians 1: 17-19).

With this insightful discerning perceptive understanding, it will no longer matter if your need is in the form of a job, a wife, a husband, fruit of the womb, or that you desire progress in your business, at work, in your relationship with your spouse, progress in the life of your children, or that you need healing, strength, divine health, or sound mind. Whatever your need, because of the concept of your perceived thought based on God's revelation, of necessity, your prayer life would become effective and productive enough to actualise those needs. This kind of prayer must not be anything short of the power of prayer prayed in faith because of the working of his mighty power that is now residual and at work in you. If for any reason, your prayer is not of faith, this means that you've not conceived your thoughts and do not believe in what you are praying about, therefore lacks the power to effect a positive change. This is because any prayer observed in doubt or in fear cannot, and will not produce results. Further to this insightful exegesis is because fear and doubt are nullifiers of faith. The Bible clarifies this thus:

> *"23...and shall not doubt in his heart, but shall believe that those things which he saith shall come to pass; he shall have whatsoever he saith. 24 Therefore I say unto you, what things so ever ye desire, when ye pray, believe that ye receive them, and ye shall have them" (Mark 11: 24).*

The scripture above relates what fear and doubt does to the human spirit; they create impossibilities which undermines your belief and subverts your faith. Letting us know that under no circumstance should you pray and allow fear and doubt cripple your faith and belief. This is why *prayer is the key in the hand of faith that opens the door of destiny.* Therefore, let the word of God through persistent power of prayer open the door of your desire whenever you pray. This means for you to receive your desire you must believe and have faith that God is who he says he is. The very essence for which prayer emphatically must be conceived by the word because *prayer is a relationship between God and* the believer that positions the believer with accurate knowledge and the understanding that God desires for his prayers to be heard and answered.

In the light of these revelation therefore, *prayer is asking with the knowledge and understanding of who God is based on his promises.* In other words, *prayer opens your life with favour for the promises of God to manifest.* This gives the believer access into God's throne room and brings him into God's set time. This is exactly what makes prayer a walk with God. It is an unceasing communion between you and God that affirms his word in times of need. *Prayer is having an understanding that God leads, guides and watches over his word when you ask and follow him in obedience.* This is because your resoluteness on God's word affirms and redefines the belief that he will never fail. And for this cause, you're being led by his Spirit to receive the object of your desire.

Let's listen once more to the prayer of Apostle Paul to the Ephesians made on behalf of all believers:

> *[17] That the God of our Lord Jesus Christ, the Father of glory, may give unto you the spirit of wisdom and revelation in the knowledge of him: [18] The eyes of your understanding being enlightened; that ye may know what is the hope of his calling, and what the riches of the glory of his inheritance in the saints, [19] And what is the exceeding greatness of his power to us-ward who believe, according to the working of his mighty power (Ephesians 1: 17-19).*

Can't you feel the move of the Spirit of God in your spirit as you're reading this book and being inundated with revelation knowledge? You are *receiving all that pertain to life and godliness;* this is the way to go, and the power of prayer will take you there.

The undisputable reality is that Apostle Paul was a man of prayer endowed with revelation knowledge and it played out in everything he did even in his prayers. This is exactly what the previewed scripture is all about; it is letting us know what are the hope of our calling and the riches of the glory of our inheritance as saints. He did not stop there, but went further to reveal the greatness of his power that is at work in us according to the working of his mighty power. So, it is his mighty power that grants every believer these revelations of the spirit. In this powerful prayer, Apostle Paul said several beautiful things of which we can carefully choose. He prayed that God may give to you the spirit of wisdom and revelation in the knowledge of him. This takes us back to the study of the word of God which will insightfully reveal the mind of God concerning the believer and what he needs to know that would enhance his relationship with God and get the believer out of trouble. This also implies that the time of trouble is when we should draw closest to God for protection and victory because many times when there's trouble; confusion sets in and seems to get a better side. This is why Apostle Paul prays for God to give all believers the spirit of wisdom and revelation in the knowledge of him. The eyes of their understanding to be enlightened so they can see hope in his calling. He is letting us know that insight into reality of what the believer should do in troubled times will help to establish peace of mind and get the believer to overcome the state of confusion or opposition. It is until you have gained spiritual wisdom, revelation knowledge and have enlightened the eyes of your understanding, and you're at peace that you can know God's mind and be able to walk in his perfect will for your life. Else, you may still be walking in confusion, fear and in doubt, thinking you're praying but your prayer is not making an impact because by doubting you're nullifying the effectiveness of your prayer with fear.

Lets liken this to a farmer who sowed his seed on thorns and is jubilating thinking he sowed on a fertile soil, expecting to reap a harvest. Of course, he will reap nothing because the thorn will not allow his seed sown in the first place to be immersed in the soil to sprout. This is because they're choked and are dead not being mixed with the fertile soul and therefore cannot produce. So also, when you are at that cross road full of quagmire, if you don't have a bearing on the word with the necessary requisites to help you in your prayer, it will be prayer prayed anxiously and in futility because fear will make it amount to nothing. So learn to pray believing and in faith, with the understanding that comes through revelation knowledge. This way the eyes of your understanding will be enlightened for you to remain resolute and immoveable on the immutable word of God. This will engender the peace that you require to keep you focused on the object of your desire, and be able to possess your possessions. And so, the Bible warns to:

> "*6Be careful for nothing; but in everything by prayer and supplication with thanksgiving let your requests be made known unto God. 7And the peace of God, which passeth all understanding, shall keep your hearts and minds through Christ Jesus (Philippians 4: 6-7).*

This scripture reinforces and equips the believer with the awareness that *prayer is a liberator that embodies both the physical and spiritual realms.* It incorporates the physical realm in the sense that it moves mountains, oppositions and meets needs, and brings healing and restoration in every fibre of the believer's being. For instance, it tells us the believer can find peace through prayer and have an unending spring of joy that will help him discover liberation in every facet of life which is why the Bible affirms.

> "*Thou wilt keep him in perfect peace, whose mind is stayed on thee: because he trusteth in thee" (Isaiah 26: 3).*

Prayer also manifests the spiritual because it reforms, transforms and conform the believer to the image of him that created him. For example, prayer keeps your spirit alert. It translates your person and helps you see life relationally from a spiritual perspective, what ordinarily you may not be able to see with your optical eyes.

> *"Praying always with all prayer and supplication in the Spirit and watching thereunto with all perseverance and supplication..."(Ephesians 6: 18).*

Prayer helps your focus and perspective to deal with the affairs of life super imposed from a higher realm, and makes you do the needful so as to accomplish purpose. This means that *prayer is the key in the hand of faith that opens the door of destiny.* Anyone's destiny can be opened with prayer. This is true because everyone born into this world is born with a destiny. However, it is incumbent on you to discover your destiny in order to walk in it and be fulfilled. This means to know God's purpose and direction for your destiny, you need to first reclaim yourself through salvation and know who you are through this liberator called *'the power of prayer.'* And as you give your heart entirely to the one that is able to do exceeding abundantly above all that you may ask or think according to his mighty power which is at work in you, then he begins to lead and orchestrate your life by his Spirit for you to discover your purpose and be fulfilled. This is because *prayer is standing resolutely and confessing what the word of God says concerning you as a result of your intimate relationship with him.* This is what activates God's mighty power in you; remember, the mighty power that is at work in you is to broaden your horizon to excel beyond the norm. That is, it will enlighten the eyes of your understanding and make you abound with revelation knowledge to approve things that are excellent and cause you to be filled with the fruits of righteousness.

> *"⁹And this I pray, that your love may abound yet more and more in knowledge and in all judgment; ¹⁰That ye may approve things that are excellent; that ye may be sincere and without offence till the day of Christ; ¹¹Being*

CHUCKS UZONWANNE

filled with the fruits of righteousness, which are by Jesus
Christ, unto the glory and praise of God" (Philippians 1:
9-11).

"²...Continue in prayer, and watch in the same with
thanksgiving; ³Withal praying also for us, that God would
open unto us a door of utterance, to speak the mystery of
Christ..." (Colossians 4: 2-3).

As a predestined child of God; who continues in prayer always sober and vigilant, you'd be able to know the purpose for your calling and also speak the mysteries of Christ because you're born of God. You are born with the spirit of purpose and of the fulfilment of destiny that reflects the glory of God. This will open the door that will usher you into God's greatness and success for your life which is why you need prayer to unveil who you are and to understand how you're to accomplish your destiny. The very reason *prayer is the key in the hand of faith that opens the door of destiny because it's believing and asking God to do through you what he has promised to do in the lives of men.*

For you to be God's vessel of honour and be led by his Spirit, you need faith to trust and believe in the word of God that God rewards diligence. Diligence and perseverance are virtues born of prayer that will help you discover your gifts to embrace your calling. This is the reason affirming who you are and fulfilling what you're called to do can only be accomplished through the power of prayer. It is also the reason why *praying in faith is unavoidable because it is God interceding on your behalf and making all things work together for your good.* At this instance, your obedience to God and love for all humanity must be inevitable. For Jesus says:

"²⁷But I say unto you which hear, Love your enemies,
do good to them which hate you, ²⁸Bless them that curse

you, and pray for them which despitefully use you (Luke 6: 27-28).

"⁴⁴...pray for them which despitefully use you, and persecute you; ⁴⁵That ye may be the children of your Father which is in heaven..." (Matthew 5: 44-45, see also 1 Samuel 12: 19-23).

Looking at the above scriptures, you tend to wonder at the complexity and the mystery of who God is. *How can you bless those who curse you and pray for those who despitefully use and persecute you?*

Someone might look at these scriptures and probably thick some as doable. For instance, you can love your enemies from afar, true; and do good to those who hate you, yes, but to bless those whom you know are enemies who not only hate you but are also cursing you is a decision of spiritual wisdom and insightful revelation knowledge. This is simply an injunction that will indeed define who you are and truly unveil your relationship with your Father which is in heaven. It's a condition that reveals your maturity and obedience to the word of God, your love for God and to all humanity without sentiments. It lets us know it is only those who hear the word in spirit and in truth that can do what it says irrespective of seeming impossibilities. In other words, you cannot do the word if you've not received the word into you. When you hear the word it needs to insightfully bring you revelation knowledge and sink into your spirit and gain residency for you to be able to do what it says. And again, Jesus is telling us that *prayer is a tool for building lives* and not destroying it. This is a task fit only for those who have surrendered their fate to God because they're blessed to be depositors of blessing in the lives of men. This invariably means that with prayer and obedience to the word of God, you can change the lives of your enemies as you do good to those who hate you, persecute and despitefully use you by emulating your Father which art in heaven. It means no one can curse he whom God has blessed because everyone that blesses you is blessed and he that curses you is cursed. Inevitably and without exception, nothing can be impossible with he who believes and adheres to the word, reason being that it rekindles your strength and generates mighty power within you to change hopeless situations.

> "*15And when Joseph's brethren saw that their father was dead, they said, Joseph will peradventure hate us, and will certainly requite us all the evil which we did unto him. 16And they sent a messenger unto Joseph, saying, Thy father did command before he died, saying, 17So shall ye say unto Joseph, Forgive, I pray thee now, the trespass of thy brethren, and their sin; for they did unto thee evil: and now, we pray thee, forgive the trespass of the servants of the God of thy father. And Joseph wept when they spake unto him. 18And his brethren also went and fell down before his face; and they said, Behold, we be thy servants. 19And Joseph said unto them, Fear not: for am I in the place of God? 20But as for you, ye thought evil against me; but God meant it unto good, to bring to pass, as it is this day, to save much people alive*" (Genesis 50: 15-20)

> "*2And I will make of thee a great nation, and I will bless thee, and make thy name great; and thou shalt be a blessing: 3And I will bless them that bless thee, and curse him that curseth thee: and in thee shall all families of the earth be blessed*" (Genesis 12: 2-3).

The brothers of Joseph meant evil for him; they lied, mistreated and sold him into slavery thinking that was going to be the end of his God given dream. But God made it work together for his good because the Lord was with him to prove his destiny. Even when they which despitefully used and sold him into slavery were at his mercy; Joseph did not hold it against them but still saved and blessed them. Therefore, be admonished and have courage to know that with prayer you can recreate your own life and that of those around you regardless of your circumstances. This is what makes you a depositor of blessing because you are Abraham's seed and this explains the reason whenever you open your mouth what comes out should be blessing. This is because you have put on the nature of God who has blessed you to be a blessing to all that encounter you. Don't be one of those who put a stumbling block in the way of others, or one of those who curse others while praying. This is because you will reap what you sow and also bear in mind that's working contrary and in disobedience to God.

> [24]*Therefore I say unto you, What things so ever ye desire, when ye pray, believe that ye receive them, and ye shall have them.* [25]*And WHEN YE STAND PRAYING, FORGIVE, if ye have ought against any: THAT YOUR FATHER ALSO WHICH IS IN HEAVEN MAY FORGIVE YOU YOUR TRESPASSES.* [26]*BUT IF YE DO NOT FORGIVE, NEITHER WILL YOUR FATHER WHICH IS IN HEAVEN FORGIVE YOUR TRESPASSES (Mark 11: 24-26).*

This scripture is simply saying that believing the word of God determines if you'll receive your desires in prayer. It also lets you know that it matters what you say when you pray because every word you utter are spiritual seeds that will abound to your spiritual bank waiting for the day of withdrawal. Another way to say it is having an understanding that *what you make happen for someone, God will make happen for you.* This also means that it is more blessed to give than to receive. Invariably, if you forgive others their trespasses, you will be forgiven also. When you do good and bless others, even those who're enemies, who hate and despitefully use you like in the case of Joseph, you'll have a harvest of your seed sown abounding to your account. *Which would you rather obey, the words of Jesus or the religions and doctrines of men?* This days you see people who gather in the name of the Lord to pray; curse their enemies and those who have offended them. And when you listen to their prayer; Satan is more pronounced than the name of the Lord. Satan this and Satan that; witches and wizards; blood of Jesus; and Holy Ghost fire! is all you hear. They have structured their mentality to Satan, witches and wizards to be more of concern to them than praising, worshipping, and praying to Almighty Jehovah. This is not the right way to pray and get the kind of result that will put you over and above your enemies. You cannot be calling Satan all the time and expect the Lord God to come to you. You cannot be seeing witches and wizards in everything and everybody and expect to walk in the grace of God. Change your mind-set and see with the vista, and the annals of God's love. The scripture says when you pray; whatever you desire and believe that you've received will become yours. But, there is a condition for your receiving it when you come before God in prayer. It is that you must:

> "...forgive, if ye have ought against any: that your Father also which is in heaven may forgive you your trespasses... (Mark 11: 25).

Understand that the reason God says to forgive is so your trespasses can also be forgiven and for your victory to be evident. When you do good and show brotherly love, distributing to the necessity even of those which persecute and despitefully use you, God comes to your defence and carries out vengeance on your behalf, heaping coals of fire upon your enemies. You become invisible to the missiles of the enemy because of the One who has taken abode in you and is fighting your battles. So, Apostle Paul having an understanding of these principles to answered prayer warns every believer to:

"⁹Let love be without dissimulation. Abhor that which is evil; cleave to that which is good...¹²Rejoicing in hope; patient in tribulation; continuing instant in prayer; ¹³Distributing to the necessity of saints; given to hospitality. ¹⁴Bless them which persecute you: bless, and curse not. ¹⁵Rejoice with them that do rejoice, and weep with them that weep...¹⁷Recompense to no man evil for evil. Provide things honest in the sight of all men. ¹⁸...live peaceably with all men. ¹⁹Dearly beloved, avenge not yourselves...for it is written, Vengeance is mine; I will repay, saith the Lord. ²⁰Therefore if thine enemy hunger, feed him; if he thirst, give him drink: for in so doing thou shalt heap coals of fire on his head. ²¹Be not overcome of evil, but overcome evil with good (Romans 12: 9, 12-21, see also proverbs 25: 21-22).

The only true way to be Christ's ambassador is through the annals of God's love. When you allow the love of God and his peace to dwell richly in your heart, you'll be able to see and relate to all men through the vista of God's love and do good; allowing God to recompense on your behalf. This is the reason a believer must not sow an evil seed, but must overcome evil with good when you:

"LET THE WORD OF CHRIST DWELL IN YOU RICHLY IN ALL WISDOM; teaching and admonishing one another..." (Colossians 3: 16)

"¹³LET US WALK HONESTLY... NOT IN STRIFE AND ENVYING. ¹⁴BUT PUT YE ON THE LORD JESUS CHRIST, AND MAKE NOT PROVISION FOR THE FLESH, TO FULFIL THE LUSTS THEREOF" (Romans 13: 13-14).

CHUCKS UZONWANNE

"⁴YE ARE OF GOD, LITTLE CHILDREN, AND HAVE OVERCOME THEM: BECAUSE GREATER IS HE THAT IS IN YOU, THAN HE THAT IS IN THE WORLD. ⁵THEY ARE OF THE WORLD: THEREFORE SPEAK THEY OF THE WORLD AND THE WORLD HEARETH THEM. ⁶WE ARE OF GOD: HE THAT KNOWETH GOD HEARETH US; HE THAT IS NOT OF GOD HEARETH NOT US. HEREBY KNOW WE THE SPIRIT OF TRUTH AND THE SPIRIT OF ERROR (1 John 4: 4-6).

These scriptures are clear on this matter, making us to understand that those who pray evil and curse others are possessed with the spirit of error. Evidently, words from the mouth of a believer are seeds sown waiting to be harvested. This means that you will reap what you sow inspite of your position however long it takes. So when God says to do good and bless your enemies and those who hate you, he means for you to reap the proceeds of your good seed sown. This means he will avenge on your behalf by heaping coals of fire upon your enemies because there is the harvest day for both good and evil, and this is God's day of vengeance when everyone will reap accordingly.

CHAPTER SEVENTEEN

THE IMPORTANCE OF PRAYER

O ur lifetime contains the only possibility required for every believer to play an active part in God's plan of salvation for humanity. This means you need to be involved and committed to the mission of saving the lost and helping them reclaim their salvation in Christ Jesus. This laudable injunction is achievable only when believers grow their faith and attach importance to prayer. And by praying agree to supplicate and intercede for lost souls that they may come to the knowledge of the truth and be saved.

"Brethren, my heart's desire and prayer to God for Israel is that they might be saved" (Romans 10: 1).

"Look unto me, and be ye saved, all the ends of the earth: for I am God, and there is none else" (Isaiah 45: 22).

The reality of this admonition reveals the importance of prayer when practised in its verity. This will translate lost souls all over the world from the powers of darkness into God's marvellous light. This can only happen when you keep abreast the mission to make the world a better place for God's righteousness to reign. This is why God is calling on everyone without reservation to look unto him and be saved. This infers that it is incumbent on every believer to arise and do the work of God while it is still day; for the night cometh when no man can work. And this can only be achieved through the witnessing of the gospel and interceding relentlessly in prayer for all to be saved.

What can be more important to a child of God than to pray and see lost souls saved? This is why *prayer is very important because it is a time of devotion with God to intercede for the lost, which is why he says to look unto him and be saved.* To accomplish God's heart desire for lost souls, prayer becomes expedient because it is through prayer that *you can talk intimately and exchange thoughts with God that will meet needs and bring his vision to reign on earth.* It is a time to ask him questions about your role in the work of expanding his kingdom on earth and what he desires to see happen in the lives of men. In the lives of those that are sick, infirmed, or diseased, and the oppressed innocent victims languishing in the prison of men, and dungeons of darkness. All of these reveal a heart given to prayer; this is the heart that knows the importance of persisting and prevailing in prayer. This heart lends it's time to meditate intercedingly on behalf of all humanity. This further reveals that the time of *prayer becomes the time to discover and harness your gifts and be a blessing to your world.* It becomes a time to learn and know how to effectively propagate the gospel and to help someone discover themselves when you lead them to Christ. It is a time to listen to instructions on all those things that are of concern to you and how you are to accomplish them. *The time of prayer is that time of meditation and fellowship with the Holy Spirit who becomes your guide to do supernaturally great and uncommon things and lead you to fulfil your destiny. This is the time when God becomes your Lord and Shepherd and leads you in the path of righteousness.* Anything you do at this instance puts on God and becomes fruitful and productive because you are walking in the footsteps of the one who is the Way, the Truth and the Life. He is the one whose name is numerous and can be called upon in spite of circumstances.

CHAPTER EIGHTEEN

DIFFERENT KINDS OF PRAYER

"I exhort therefore, that, first of all, supplications, prayers, intercessions, and giving of thanks, be made for all men" (1 Timothy 2: 1).

There are different kinds of prayer, of which we would consider four:

1. PRAYER OF SUPPLICATION

The prayer of supplication is the prayer of request. Supplication is the same in meaning as request, asking or petition; and will be used interchangeably. This kind of prayer deals with asking for something politely or formally without begging. We must understand and settle it in our hearts that there is a difference between asking for something and begging for something. If you know who you are as a child of God, that is, the authority you have been vested with in Christ, then you will understand that ASKING EMPOWERS YOU while BEGGING MAKES YOU INSIGNIFICANT.

[20]Neither for these alone do I pray [ask] (it is not for their sake only that I make this request), but also for all

those who will ever come to believe in (trust in, cling to, rely on) me through their word and teaching [when we propagate the gospel and call an assembly]. ²¹That they all may be one, (just) as you, Father, are in Me and I in You, that they also may be one in Us, so that the world may believe and be convinced that You have sent Me. ²²I have given to them the glory and honour which You have given Me, that they may be one (even) as We are one: ²³I in them and You in Me, in order that they may become one and perfectly united, that the world may know and (definitely) recognize that You sent Me and that You have loved them (even) as You have loved Me. ²⁴Father, I desire (request) that they also whom You have entrusted to Me (as Your gift to Me) may be with Me where I am, so that they may see My glory, which you have given Me (Your love gift to Me); for You loved Me before the foundation of the world (John 17: 20 -24 Amp). Emphasis mine

This scripture reveals that Jesus prayed not only for his disciples but also for every believer in generations to come. *Why did Jesus pray for all believers?* Jesus prayed for all believers because his desire is for them to love one another and be united in him just as he is united with the Father. The essence is so he and the Father can take abode in every believer for the whole world to be convinced and believe that God has sent him and he in turn has sent us because of who he is. His request is for the Father's love to be extended to all believers through him and wants all those who believe in him to be with him and see his glory. This is a prayer of request to the Father on behalf of all believers. When Jesus prayed this prayer we were not there but he had every believer in mind as he prayed to the Father.

What is prayer of request?

Going by the above scripture and explanations, *the prayer of request is asking for something from someone either for you or on behalf of another.* For instance, Jesus prayed to the Father for every believer to love one another that the world may be convinced of whom he is and also wants every believer to be with him so they can see his glory. This explains that *the prayer of request or supplication is when you present to God the things you want him to do for you or for someone else that may not be there or know that you have prayed for them. Another example is the case of Hannah:*

> *And she was in bitterness of soul, and prayed unto the Lord, and wept sore. And she vowed a vow, and said, O Lord of hosts, if thou wilt indeed look on the affliction of thine handmaid, and remember me, and not forget thine handmaid, BUT WILL GIVE UNTO THINE HANDMAID A MAN CHILD, THEN I WILL GIVE HIM UNTO THE LORD ALL THE DAYS OF HIS LIFE, and there shall no razor come upon his head (1 Samuel 1: 10 – 11; see also Esther 4: 7 - 17).*

Picture this scenario of a woman distressed and in bitterness of soul. Her situation was such that no one else could help her, but God alone. And so, she prayed and wept before the Lord, vowing as she made her supplication. *And what was her supplication?* She asked the Lord for a man child whom she will give back to serve the Lord all the days of his life. The beauty of this supplication is that the person being prayed for [Samuel] was not there. And the Lord heard and granted her request as she in turn fulfilled her vow. For those that are living in the dispensation of the grace of our Lord Jesus Christ, always remember that when you stand before God with your prayer request, it has to be in the name of Jesus. *Why is this so?* This is so because the name of Jesus is every believer's access to the Father; and the Holy Spirit responds only to the name of Jesus. This is the reason the Bible says,

> "And whatsoever ye shall ask in my name [in the name of Jesus], that will I do [Jesus will do], that the Father may be glorified in the Son [Jesus]. If ye shall ask any thing in my name, I will do it" (John 14: 13 see also John 14: 26 & 15: 26). Emphasis mine

This is an indication that the prayer of request is asking for something either for self or on behalf of another in the name of Jesus.

> Verily, verily, I say unto you, whatsoever YE SHALL ASK THE FATHER IN MY NAME, He will give it you. Hitherto have ye asked nothing in my name: ask, and ye shall receive, that your joy may be full (John 16: 23 - 24).

Having observed the above scripture in this case, will it not be an insult to come before God in the name of Jesus and be begging? No one who comes in the name of Jesus should condescend to the beggarly life however complex the circumstance. You're to ask only, and that must be with the knowledge and understanding of the rights you have in Christ. *Understand that when you ask in the name of Jesus, the angels in heaven are paying attention and God is listening to your supplication and watching to recognise your presentation, composure and boldness. And also the Holy Spirit is waiting willingly to respond to your request made in the name of Jesus.* This is because the name of Jesus is the name above all names; recognised in heaven, in the earth, beneath the earth, and in the seas.

> *9Wherefore God also hath highly exalted Him, and given Him a name which is above every name: 10That at the name of Jesus every knee should bow, of things in*

heaven, and things in earth, and things under the earth;
¹¹And that every tongue should confess that Jesus Christ
is Lord, to the glory of God the Father (Philippians 2:
9 – 11).

Because the name of Jesus is your access to God the Father, when you stand before God to make your request, he does not see you as insignificant, worthless and sinful people. God sees Jesus in you because you are standing in the stead of Jesus before him. This means *God does not see you for what you were but who you are in Christ; sinless, blameless and righteous before him.*

> *Therefore if any man be in Christ, he is a new creature:*
> *old things are passed away; behold all things are become*
> *new (2 Corinthians 5: 17).*

2. PRAYER OF INTERCESSION

The prayer of intercession is prayer observed by an individual or a group of people on behalf of someone, a nation or the world; and these may be oblivious of the individual or group of people praying. For example, in soul winning, the prayer of intercession is required and very necessary because it acts as a major factor in consideration. An instance is when the Bible says *"Ask of me, and I shall give thee the heathen for thine inheritance, and the uttermost parts of the earth for thy possession" (Psalm 2: 8; see also Ezekiel 18: 4).* This means to stand in the gap for someone, to intervene for a nation or intercede for the world. Your reason for interceding is so they can be saved. *The prayer of intercession is for the salvation and benefit of someone or a group of people without their knowing or consent.* And unless of course, the person is told or specifically requested that the prayer of intercession be made on their behalf will the person know straightaway that he's being prayed for. An example is when God visited Abraham in Genesis 18, God asked Abraham to intercede for Sodom in order to prevent him from destroying it. Abraham took it upon himself to intercede for Sodom because of his nephew Lot who at the time before its destruction lived in Sodom. Lot was not aware that Abraham interceded on his behalf; it was for the sake of Abraham's intercession that Lot was spared.

> *²⁰And the Lord said, because the cry of Sodom and Gomorrah is great, and because their sin is very grievous; ²¹I will go down now, and see whether they have done altogether according to the cry of it, which is come unto me; and if not, I will know. ²²And the men turned their faces from thence, and went toward Sodom: but Abraham stood yet before the Lord. ²³And Abraham drew near, and said, wilt thou also destroy the righteous with the wicked? ²⁴Peradventure there be fifty righteous within the city: wilt thou also destroy and not spare the place for the fifty righteous that are therein? ²⁵That be far from thee to do after this manner, to slay the righteous with the wicked: and that the righteous should be as the wicked, that be far from thee: shall not the judge of all the earth do right? ²⁶And the Lord said, if I find in Sodom fifty righteous within the city; then I will spare all the place for their sakes. ²⁷And Abraham answered and said, behold now, I have taken upon me to speak unto the Lord, which am but dust and ashes: ²⁸Peradventure there shall lack five of the fifty righteous: wilt thou destroy all the city for lack of five? And He said, if I find there forty and five, I will not destroy it. ²⁹And he spake unto Him yet again, and said, peradventure there shall be forty found there. And He said, I will not do it for forty's sake. ³⁰And he said unto Him, oh let not the Lord be angry, and I will speak: peradventure there shall thirty be found there. And He said, I will not do it, if I find thirty there. ³¹And he said, behold now, I have taken upon me to speak unto the Lord: peradventure there*

shall be twenty found there. And He said, I will not destroy it for twenty's sake. ³²And he said, oh let not the Lord be angry, and I will speak yet but this once: peradventure ten shall be found there. And He said, I will not destroy it for ten's sake.

³³And the Lord went His way, as soon as He had left communing with Abraham: and Abraham returned unto his place (Genesis 18: 20 – 33; see also Jonah 1: 1 - 2).

Admittedly, one can deduce that *an intercessor is one who stands in the gap between God and man to mediate on their behalf in prayer.* The Bible says,

"Ask of me, and I shall give thee the heathen for thine inheritance, and the uttermost parts of the earth for thy possession (Psalm 2: 8).

In this instance, God is instructing the intercessors to ask for the salvation of the people [nations]. If God is asking for the intercession of the people which means that *the prayer of intercession is necessary and an essential tool without which soul winning will be an exercise in futility.*

To win a soul is to prevent and deliver from sin; save a soul from destruction and from going to hell. This is because man is a spirit and can only be reformed or related to spiritually. Man is related to spiritually because sin is a spirit that separates men from God and becomes a reproach and leads men to hell. This is why man needs to be saved, and your intercessory prayer will help save someone from going to hell. This is because heaven and hell are real and can only be attained spiritually. This is the reason you have been vested with the responsibility to intercede by asking for the souls of men before they are damned in hell.

The Bible says, "It is appointed unto man once to die and after death comes judgement" (Hebrews 9: 27). For all have sinned, and come short of the glory of God (Romans 3: 23; see Ezekiel 18: 4).

The prayer of intercession is very similar to the prayer of request but not exactly the same. The prayer of request is asking for the benefit of you or others who may not be there when you are praying for them (John 17: 20 – 24; 1 Samuel 1: 10 – 11), while prayer of intercession is standing in the gap [to mediate, to prevent, or save] in prayer for others also who may or may not be aware unless they specifically requested for you to intercede in prayer for them (Genesis 18: 20 – 33). For instance:

⁵Peter therefore was kept in prison: but prayer was made without ceasing of the church unto God for him...¹²And when he [Peter] had considered the thing, he came to the house of Mary the mother of John, whose surname was Mark; where MANY WERE GATHERED TOGETHER PRAYING [for him] (Acts 12: 5, 12) Emphasis mine.

In this instance, Peter was unaware that the Church at Mary's house was interceding for him. It was as a result of the prayer of intercession by the Church that moved the angel of the Lord to rescue Peter from the prison against the wicked desires of the Jews and the plan of Herod.

3. PRAYER OF AGREEMENT

The prayer of agreement is two or more people consenting concerning a matter. This means they're praying in harmony or in one accord regarding an issue. This could be on behalf of someone who may or may not be aware also that he is being prayed for. The person might be involved with those who are consenting in prayer. This kind of prayer is usually between two or more people praying in consonance for themselves, or someone making a request for those praying to intercede for someone concerning an objective or common goal. Before Jesus ascended into heaven, after his resurrection, he showed himself alive to his disciples for forty days and taught them pertaining to the kingdom of God.

He commanded them that they should not depart from Jerusalem, but to wait for the promise of the Father, which he spoke to them about concerning their endowment or being baptized with the Holy Spirit to enable them witness effectively. After these instructions Jesus was taken up into heaven. When they returned to Jerusalem from the Mount of Olives they went up into an upper room and the Bible let us know what they were gathered doing:

All of these with their minds in FULL AGREEMENT (continued with one accord, joined together) devoted themselves steadfastly (constantly) to prayer (Acts 1: 14).

They were praying the prayer of agreement based on the revelation giving to them on the Mount of Olives concerning their being endowed with the Holy Spirit according to the words of Jesus. All of those who gathered in the upper room devoted themselves steadfastly to prayer. Their minds were knitted together in one accord, in full agreement with their resolve, the instructions they have received from our Lord Jesus to stay in Jerusalem until they were baptized with the Holy Spirit. And so, they began to pray the prayer of agreement waiting daily for the outpouring of the Holy Spirit as they were promised until the day of Pentecost when they were all filled with the Holy Spirit and began to speak in other languages as the Holy Spirit gave them utterance. The Holy Spirit was given to them for empowerment to enable them witness with strong conviction. This we see in Peter who stood up with the eleven with boldness to address the crowd of people who had gathered, and it became an opportunity for him to witness to the people:

> *Then they that gladly received his word were baptized: and the same day there were added unto them about three thousand souls. And they continued steadfastly in the apostles' doctrine and fellowship, and in breaking of bread, and in prayers (Acts 2: 41 – 42).*

After they gladly received the word and were baptized, they adhered to the apostle's doctrine and devoted themselves to fellowship and prayer. Meaning they were all in agreement: no wonder when Peter was put in prison, they were able to gather and agree in prayer as was their custom:

> *[12]And when he (Peter) had considered the thing, he came to the house of Mary the mother of John, whose surname was Mark; where many were gathered together praying (Acts 12: 12).*

When you hold someone's hand, or say to someone, *"Let us pray"* for a brother, a sister, the needs in Church, those that are sick in hospitals, innocent souls in prison all over the world, those on the mission field, widows, orphans, someone's business, what goes on in their place of work, your community, leaders of nations, friends, siblings or for yourselves regarding your wife, husband, children, relationship with others, marriage, counsel or any matters arising; you are compelling them to pray the prayer of request, agreement or intercession because you are both consenting in agreement to someone's request dependent on whatever you are praying about for those you're interceding for; who're oblivious of your prayers. This is why the Bible says to pray for one another, knowing that:

"The earnest heartfelt, continued prayer of a righteous man makes tremendous power available; it is dynamic in its working" (James 5: 16).

Again I say unto you, that IF TWO OF YOU SHALL AGREE on earth as touching anything that THEY SHALL ASK, it shall be done for them of my Father which is in heaven (Matthew 18: 19).

The scripture above reveals the mind of Christ regarding prayer of agreement, reason being that two cannot walk together except they are in agreement, for where two are in agreement tremendous power is made available which is why Jesus said, *"if two of you shall agree on earth as touching anything you shall ask"* it shall be answered and brought to manifestation by God because you are persistently exercising the power of prayer in agreement and in faith. This means that when believers pray in agreement, it positions them to receive answers to their prayers as long as they are walking in God's perfect will. As a believer, you must not relent in making your requests known when you intercede and agree with others in prayer.

4. PRAYER OF THANKSGIVING

Why do we give thanks? We give thanks to show our gratitude for what has been done for us or what we are about to receive in anticipation of our request. And so, *the prayer of thanksgiving is the prayer of appreciation and of gratitude.* God wants us to be appreciative of who we are, by humbly showing gratitude for what we have and where we are in life. And with our humble thankful attitude he improves our lives, promoting and positioning us for greater heights of success.

The prayer of thanksgiving encourages us to give God thanks in everything, regardless of what the circumstances may be. This is the reason the Bible enjoins us to:

> [16]*Be joyful always;* [17]*pray continually;* [18]*give thanks in all circumstances, for this is God's will for you in Christ Jesus (1 Thessalonians 5: 16 – 18; see also Ephesians 5: 20; 1 Corinthians 15: 57 & 2 Corinthians 2: 14; Hebrews 13: 15).*

How do we give thanks? We give thanks by appreciating God in all circumstances. When we come before God, the foremost thing any believer should do; is to worship God for who he is; in Spirit and in truth, praising him in songs and in hymns, making melody in our hearts to him. That is, being joyful in his presence and reminding him of his goodness and promises, thanking him for hearing and answering our prayer.

> *"Speaking to yourselves in psalms and hymns and spiritual songs, singing and making melody in your heart to the Lord; giving thanks always for all things unto God and the Father in the name of our Lord Jesus Christ" (Ephesians 5: 19 – 20; see also Psalm 100: 4; 95: 2; 107: 1).*

Whatever we are praying for that is according to God's perfect will, has a guarantee we will have it when we joyfully thank him for it in the name of Jesus because it is his will for us that our prayers be answered. This reminds us that when we pray, we should always give thanks and be joyful with the understanding that God hears us, because this is his will for those in Christ Jesus. The Bible says:

"Do not be anxious about anything, but in everything, by prayer and petition, WITH THANKSGIVING, present your requests to God" (Philippians 4: 6).

This further goes to explain why some people pray and don't receive from God because of anxiety, lack of appreciation, and not coming before him in the name of Jesus. And so the Bible encourages every believer to give God thanks always, and not to be anxious about anything because anxiety is a faith destroyer. It breeds fear and make you want to question the word of God because at that moment you're walking in the flesh; in your senses and seeing the wrong things and this makes you a double-minded person.

A double-minded person wavers in his opinion, and that shows his lack of faith and therefore cannot receive from God. You must not belong to this group of persons, who lack knowledge of the word of God. Be a doer of the word and stand firmly on the word through the persistent prevailing power of prayer. This will free you from bondage and cause your spirit to sower above your circumstances and make you walk in victory and dominion. Remember that with prayer nothing shall be impossible unto him that believes.

CHUCKS UZONWANNE

PRAYER EXERCISE

1. Why did Jesus pray for all believers?

_____

_____

_____

2. What is the essence of this prayer?

_____

_____

_____

3. What is this kind of prayer called?

_____

4. What book of the gospel is this prayer located?

_____

5. Name four kinds of prayers?

_____

_____

_____

_____

CHAPTER NINETEEN

THE PRINCIPLES OF PRAYER

"AND ALL THINGS, WHATSOEVER, YOU SHALL ASK IN PRAYER, BELIEVING YOU SHALL RECEIVE THEM" (Matthew 21: 22).

The preview above reveals the three principles of prayer. The foremost principle of prayer is:

1. ASK

This principle is the determining principle without which prayer will be futile. It powerfully positions you with choices anticipating your possession. At the instance when your resolve is to ask for something, it automatically registers in your subconscious and paints the picture of the very object of your desire. This leaves you with the decision of the time you want it and how, when and where you want it. This is the key to anyone's receiving in faith because it ensures the maintenance of the right focus and perspective. This also shows that for you to ask you must first predicate your resolve on the object of your desire to know if it is something you need and if it is urgently important that you have it.

Do you know that the easiest thing anyone can do is to ask? Yet, it is not as easy as it sounds because it is one thing to ask for something, and an entirely different thing to believe for what you have asked for. *What do I mean?* Obviously, many ask without being specific and having a cogent reason because they don't believe that they can have it. So they ask for asking sake seeing every other person is asking for the same thing. If you ask them to explain why they are asking for what they have asked for, they will tell you they don't know but they want it. For instance, someone might purchase a latest brand new car and see it as luxury because he can afford it and has many others parked in his garage. These cars in his garage serve different occasion while some other person who bought his first car see it as a necessity to meet urgently important needs. This means that the person who bought his first car must put into consideration certain factors such as cost of maintenance at the backdrop of other expenses to resolve the value of need. If he wants to be like the one who purchased the latest brand new car and sees his first and only car as luxury and decides to recruit a chauffeur and pleasurably drive the car around without being able to pay his driver and maintain the car, then it's purpose is defeated because he can't afford it and doesn't need it. This is why people don't have an idea or a clue to what they want, they just want it because everybody else is asking for it and so they want it too. Or sometimes, they just want it to prove they can have it, but not because it is essentially needed or urgently important. Don't be like that, this is because you're different and a child of God. This further means that *you're asking must be to meet urgent and important need in consonance with the will of God for you.* This relates for us to know there is a difference between wanting something because everybody wants it and needing something because it will help you become better, bless someone and give glory to God. So you can see that many ask for things they don't have need of and this is the reason why:

- *They cannot believe in what they're asking for because it lacks importance.*

- *There is no value attached to it.*
- *It is only at the instance of a need that you're asking becomes valued and relevant to you.*

Let me explain further, of course, you're aware there is a difference between a need and a want.

A need is 'now' to meet an urgent and important obligation while a want is gratification of the flesh. If you scale your preference, you will understand what a need is different from what a want is. It is when you have a need that you can believe and your asking becomes relevant to you because of the value placed on the need. This motivates you to ask in faith because you now believe. What this does is that it puts your faith into action. For instance, some people don't believe in miracles, some don't believe in healing and some don't believe in prayer because they don't believe in God. You will be amazed at what some people don't believe in, but at the instance when they are sick or infirmed and they now have a special need for healing and a miracle that is when they believe there is God. Because they now have a need beyond their control, you will see them running from pillar to post and are willing to move any mountain in order to meet such needs. You must realise for that need to be met, firstly, you must believe; and for you to believe, you must ask in faith. It is at the point of asking that it all begins to work in your favour because you not only believe but now you're acting on your believe and can receive in faith.

2. BELIEVE

To believe is to have a reposed confidence in God. This means to trust in the word of God; to acknowledge that God exists and see him as real, and always true to his word. This further implies that *'believe' is insightful and revelatory in nature because it deals with the qualities which identify with the personality of God. This makes belief the most important principle of the power of prayer!* You must believe for you to be able to ask; and you must believe to act in faith. You must believe that when you ask in faith God hears and will answer whenever you pray. When someone believes in the word of God, regardless of the circumstances, 'all things' becomes his as he discovers his faith is activated and this positions him to receive what he has asked for because his faith is working. Look at the scripture once again and ponder on it carefully acting on your belief. Can you see that it says:

> "And all things, whatsoever, you shall ask for in prayer, BELIEVING YOU SHALL RECEIVE THEM" (Matthew 21: 22).

Can you see what I see here, did it say "BELIEVING and you shall RECEIVE..." This is insightfully deep, and I tell you, if you miss it here, you miss it all! It is imperative at this instance that you be meticulous, cautious concerning minute details and pay particular attention to what I'm about to show you because this lets us know that when you believe nothing shall be impossible to you. Your strong belief at the point of your resolve to ask will dispel fear and doubt and make impossibilities to be estranged in your life. This will help your resoluteness on the word of God because your believing now positions your faith to receive the object of your desire at the instance when you have prayed. *How do I mean?* At this instance when you believe you have something, you are convinced it is yours because you can see it and so you believe it's yours for possession. And for you to see it you must see it with the eyes of the spirit. Although it is yet to manifest physically but because you believe strongly it's yours, you will have it. This is because the tangibility of the manifestation is dependent on what you see and have claimed in the realms of the spirit. And faith is what you need to see with the eyes of the spirit to claim it's yours by calling it forth and making it a reality.

This instructs that *'Faith' is any minute and every minute believer who calls forth things that be not as though they already exists.* Further reveals that *faith is seeing the unseen. It is the reality of the spirit world!*

Faith is crucial in our work with God if we must have effective prayer life and experience the power of prayer. This is so, because faith is another important principle of the power of prayer which reveals that at the point of believing when you ask, your faith is energized and activated and goes into action for possession. This relates that *faith is the messenger of your belief because it is activated and goes to bring the object of your desire to your spirit's conviction and makes it real.* You must understand that *without believing there is no faith, and without faith you cannot receive. Therefore, we need faith at all times to effectively pray and positively affect our prayer life to receive answers.* For instance, if someone who believes in the healing power of God were sick; for him to receive his healing and miracles, he must believe and have faith that he can be healed by standing resolutely on the promises of God as it relates to his healing. He must apply his faith at the instance when he prays and believes that God is not only able but also willing to heal him. Therefore, he must position and align himself with his believing to receive in faith. For this to happen, he needs to research the scriptures on the subject that relates to faith and apply the relevant to his condition by confessing what the word of God says and seeing his healing in the mirror of his faith.

The Bible says in Psalm 107: 20, *"He sent his word, and healed them, and delivered them from their destructions."*

With this inference, we should ask *"How did God send His word to heal and deliver from destruction?* The foremost is to understand that the word of God is God, and God is Spirit. This reveals to us God's Holy Presence known as the Holy Spirit. The Holy Spirit of God is the Angel of his presence who only responds to the spoken word of God. The Holy Spirit is a person and doer of God's spoken word. This makes God Omniscient because he is everywhere but his manifested presence is only where he's welcomed. It is until you call to God that his Holy Presence manifests and are felt.

> For where two or three are gathered together in my name, there am I in the midst of them (Matthew 18:20).

I know you are surprised to hear that God is everywhere but his manifested presence is not, unless you call to him. Having a clear understanding of this revelation is the first step to the journey of the Power of Prayer. This is why he is able to heal and to deliver from destruction those who call on him. The insight to this revelation is in John chapter one and from verse one:

> *In the beginning was the Word, and the Word was with God, and the Word was God. *The same was in the beginning with God. *All things were made by him; and without him was not anything made that was made. *In him was life; and the life was the light of men. *And the light shineth in darkness; and the darkness comprehended it not (John 1: 1 – 5).

The revelation here is saying that the word which God sent to heal and deliver his children from destruction was with him from the beginning of time, and all things were made by him. He is the Eternal Life and the Light of men with whom we can see through our dark world. He is the light that shined away darkness at the hour of creation in Genesis chapter one and verses one to three.

> *That was the true Light, which lighteth every man that cometh into the world. *He was in the world, and the world was made by him, and the world knew him not. *He came unto his own, and his own received him not.

¹²BUT AS MANY AS RECEIVED HIM, TO THEM GAVE HE POWER TO BECOME THE SONS OF GOD, EVEN TO THEM THAT BELIEVE ON HIS NAME: ¹³WHICH WERE BORN, NOT OF BLOOD, NOR OF THE WILL OF THE FLESH, NOR OF THE WILL OF MAN, BUT OF GOD (John 1: 9 – 13).

The word is the true Light who radiates every man that is born into the kingdom of God because they received him and believed in his name. He gave them the ability to overcome sickness and every destructive tendencies, because they are now the sons of God; reason being these sons of God are not born of blood that can be corrupted with sickness, disease, or infirmity nor do they reason with their senses. Neither do they see with their optical eyes but with the eyes of the Spirit which is the eyes of faith because they are sons in the kingdom of God.

> *¹⁴And the Word was made flesh, and dwelt among us, (and we beheld his glory, the glory as of the only begotten of the Father,) full of grace and truth... ¹⁸No man hath seen God at any time; the only begotten Son, which is in the bosom of the Father, he hath declared him (John 1: 14 & 18).*

The begotten Son declared who the Father is because the Son is the spoken word of the Father who came into the world to fulfil the word of the Father by healing and delivering from destruction *(Acts 10: 38)*. When the word came into the world, he came through a virgin named Mary. He was not born of the will of the flesh, nor of the will of man because he has no biological explanation. The Holy Spirit of God overshadowed Mary and she conceived fulfilling the words of prophecy. See what Matthew and Luke wrote about it; *Luke 1: 26 - 35; Matthew 1: 18 - 23:*

26And in the sixth month the angel Gabriel was sent from God unto a city of Galilee, named Nazareth, 27To a virgin espoused to a man whose name was Joseph, of the house of David; and the virgin's name was Mary. 28And the angel came in unto her, and said, Hail, thou that art highly favoured, the Lord is with thee: blessed art thou among women. 29And when she saw him, she was troubled at his saying, and cast in her mind what manner of salutation this should be. 30And the angel said unto her, Fear not, Mary: for thou hast found favour with God. 31And, behold, thou shalt conceive in thy womb, and bring forth a son, and shalt call his name JESUS. 32He shall be great, and shall be called the Son of the Highest: and the Lord God shall give unto him the throne of his father David: 33And he shall reign over the house of Jacob for ever; and of his kingdom there shall be no end. 34Then said Mary unto the angel, How shall this be, seeing I know not a man? 35And the angel answered and said unto her, the Holy Ghost shall come upon thee, and the power of the Highest shall overshadow thee: therefore also that holy thing which shall be born of thee shall be called the Son of God (Luke 1: 26 – 35).

18Now the birth of Jesus Christ was on this wise: When as his mother Mary was espoused to Joseph, before they came together, she was found with child of the Holy Ghost. 19Then Joseph her husband, being a just man, and not willing to make her a publick example, was minded to put her away privily. 20But while he thought on these things, behold, the angel of the Lord appeared unto him in a dream, saying, Joseph, thou son of David, fear not to take unto thee Mary thy wife: for that which is conceived in her is of the Holy Ghost. 21And she shall bring forth a son and thou shalt call his name JESUS: for he shall save his people from their sins.

²²Now all this was done, that it might be fulfilled which was spoken of the Lord by the prophet, saying, ²³Behold, a virgin shall be with child, and shall bring forth a son, and they shall call his name Emmanuel, which being interpreted is, God with us (Matthew 1: 18 – 23; see also Isaiah 7: 14).

We can now understand clearly that when God sent his word, he gave him a name for identification. This is to fulfil the words of the prophets and to prove that the creator-word is in the world. There were signs to authenticate the fulfilment of the word of God *"He sent his word, and healed them, and delivered them from their destructions"(Psalm 107: 20)*. There were many infallible prove that the word which God spoke in the Garden of Eden at the fall of man was fulfilled in Jesus Christ.

¹⁶And he withdrew himself into the wilderness, and prayed. ¹⁷And it came to pass on a certain day, as he was teaching, that there were Pharisees and doctors of the law sitting by, which were come out of every town of Galilee, and Judaea, and Jerusalem: and the power of the Lord was present to heal them (Luke 5: 16 – 17; see also Matthew 4: 23 - 24; 8: 15 - 17; 9: 27 - 33; Mark 1: 21 - 27, 32 - 35).

This scripture is revealing the life style of Jesus and the importance of the Power of prayer. Jesus withdrew himself to a solitary place in the wilderness where he can meditate and pray. He also taught the word of God to the people and preached the gospel of the kingdom; and bam! The power of the Lord was present to heal the people.

CHUCKS UZONWANNE

²³And Jesus went about all Galilee, teaching in their synagogues, and preaching the gospel of the kingdom, and healing all manner of sickness and all manner of disease among the people. ²⁴And his fame went throughout all Syria: and they brought unto him all sick people that were taken with divers diseases and torments, and those which were possessed with devils, and those which were lunatick, and those that had the palsy; and he healed them (Matthew 4: 23 – 24).

How did God send his word? He sent his word through Jesus his Son. *How did Jesus deliver the world from destruction and bring healing?* We must be aware that without the shedding of blood, there is no remission of sins *[Hebrews 9: 22]*. The word of God, Jesus became the Lamb of God who came into the world to take away the sins of the world *[John 1: 29; 17: 24; Proverbs 8: 22 - 31; Isaiah 53: 7; 1 Peter 1: 18 - 20]. How was he able to accomplish these?* Because Jesus is God; His blood was without contamination and sin *[2 Corinthians 5: 18, 19, 21 Refer to Miracle of the New Birth]*.

¹⁸And all things are of God, who hath reconciled us to himself by Jesus Christ...¹⁹To wit, that God was in Christ, reconciling the world unto himself, not imputing their trespasses unto them; and hath committed unto us the word of reconciliation... ²¹For he hath made him to be sin for us, who knew no sin; that we might be made the righteousness of God in him (2 Corinthians 5: 18, 19 & 22).

How did he do it? Firstly, he had to die by shedding his own blood for the sins of the world and became the perfect sacrifice for all humanity. There remaineth no more sacrifice for sin. The Bible gives us more insight:

^{6}Now when these things were thus ordained, the priests went always into the first tabernacle, accomplishing the service of God. ^{7}But into the second went the high priest alone once every year, not without blood, which he offered for himself, and for the errors of the people:

^{8}The Holy Ghost this signifying, that the way into the holiest of all was not yet made manifest, while as the first tabernacle was yet standing: ^{9}Which was a figure for the time then present, in which were offered both gifts and sacrifices, that could not make him that did the service perfect, as pertaining to the conscience; ^{10}Which stood only in meats and drinks, and divers washings, and carnal ordinances, imposed on them until the time of reformation. ^{11}But Christ being come an high priest of good things to come, by a greater and more perfect tabernacle, not made with hands, that is to say, not of this building; ^{12}Neither by the blood of goats and calves, but by his own blood he entered in once into the holy place, having obtained eternal redemption for us. ^{13}For if the blood of bulls and of goats, and the ashes of an heifer sprinkling the unclean, sanctifieth to the purifying of the flesh: ^{14}How much more shall the blood of Christ, who through the eternal Spirit offered himself without spot to God, purge your conscience from dead works to serve the living God? ^{15}And for this cause he is the mediator of the new testament, that by means of death, for the redemption of the transgressions that were under the first testament, they which are called might receive the promise of eternal inheritance. ^{16}For where a testament is, there must also of necessity be the death of the testator. ^{17}For a testament is of force after men are dead: otherwise it is of no strength at all while the testator liveth. ^{18}Whereupon neither the first testament was dedicated without blood. ^{19}For when Moses had spoken every precept to all the people according to the

CHUCKS UZONWANNE

law, he took the blood of calves and of goats, with water, and scarlet wool, and hyssop, and sprinkled both the book, and all the people, [20]Saying, this is the blood of the testament which God hath enjoined unto you. [21]Moreover he sprinkled with blood both the tabernacle and all the vessels of the ministry. [22]And almost all things are by the law purged with blood; and without shedding of blood is no remission. [23]It was therefore necessary that the patterns of things in the heavens should be purified with these; but the heavenly things themselves with better sacrifices than these. [24]For Christ is not entered into the holy places made with hands, which are the figures of the true; but into heaven itself, now to appear in the presence of God for us: [25]NOR YET THAT HE SHOULD OFFER HIMSELF OFTEN, AS THE HIGH PRIEST ENTERETH INTO THE HOLY PLACE EVERY YEAR WITH BLOOD OF OTHERS; [26]For then must he often have suffered since the foundation of the world: but now once in the end of the world hath he appeared to put away sin by the sacrifice of himself. [27]And as it is appointed unto men once to die, but after this the judgment: [28]So Christ was once offered to bear the sins of many; and unto them that look for him shall he appear the second time without sin unto salvation (Hebrews 9: 6 – 28).

[15]And that he died for all, that they which live should not henceforth live unto themselves, but unto him which died for them, and rose again...[18]And all things are of God, who hath reconciled us to himself by Jesus Christ...; [19]To wit, that GOD WAS IN CHRIST, RECONCILING THE WORLD UNTO HIMSELF, NOT IMPUTING THEIR TRESPASSES UNTO THEM...;[21]For he hath made him to be sin for us, who knew no sin; that we might be made the righteousness of God in him (2 Corinthians 5: 15, 18, 19 & 21).

He took our place and our sins were laid upon his Spirit; He is the Lamb that was slain from the foundation of the world. When Jesus died, every believer and all those who believed for salvation before his advent died with him, when he rose from the dead, every believer rose with him, a new specie of being without sin and without a past, which is why the Bible says,

> *"if any man be in Christ, he is a new creation, old things are passed away, behold, all things are become new"* (2 Corinthians 5: 17).

This also means that those who received the Word have been empowered with the ability to speak in his name and recreate circumstances for their own good. So, the believer must see his healing and have faith in the power of prayer by believing that God heard him and wishes for him to be healed because his healing was perfected by the word, *"with the stripes of Jesus he has been healed"* [1 Peter 2: 24; Isaiah 53: 5]. He must believe with every fibre of his being that Jesus bore his sickness and infirmity irrespective of his physical condition despite what his senses dictate, he must believe that he is healed and begin to thank God for his healing, acting as the healed as he sees himself being healed. This is when his faith becomes operational and effective.

3. RECEIVE

To receive is to accept or acknowledge the manifested reality of the object of your desire predicated on your asking and believing. Evidently, for you to receive you must ask and believe in yourself that what you have asked for is yours because you believe in the word of God that his word will not return without accomplishing what it talks about. This means that you have confidence that once you can affirm in your spirit what the word of God says concerning the object of your desire; knowing it is in consonance with his will then it is yours to receive. This is implying that having done all there is to do; the next available thing is to receive. At this point, it is yours for the taking because you can see it tangibly in manifestation.

CHAPTER TWENTY

PRAYER THROUGH FAITH IN THE WORD

T here is the need to pray and have faith in the word of God by resolutely believing that God will hear and answer your prayers. And this cannot be over-emphasised because we know that Jesus Christ is the same yesterday, today and forever (Hebrews 13: 8). Jesus is here now, if you would believe and cry out to him in prayer by faith. He will hear and bring healing in every area of your life because his desire is for you to be healed and walk in greatness and in success. These are his thoughts for you!

> *[21]Jesus answered and said unto them, verily I say unto you, if you have faith, and doubt not, you shall not only do this which is done to the fig tree, but also IF YOU SHALL SAY UNTO THIS MOUNTAIN, BE THOU REMOVED, AND BE THOU CAST INTO THE SEA; IT SHALL BE DONE. [22]AND ALL THINGS, WHATSOEVER YOU SHALL ASK IN PRAYER, BELIEVING YOU SHALL RECEIVE (Matthew 21: 21 – 22).*

This scripture reveals the power of prayer through faith in the word: *[21]...if you shall say unto this mountain, be thou removed, and be thou cast into the sea; it shall be done. ²²and all things, whatsoever you shall ask in prayer, believing you shall receive...* It tells you that prayer and faith in the word of God are the prerequisites you need to change any hopeless situation and pull down mountains. Mountain in this context signifies problems – troubles of life such as: sickness, infirmity, disease, lack, poverty, unproductiveness, confusion, contention, limitation, stagnation, etc. Anything and everything that is opposed to the word of God manifesting in your life for you to live a fruitful and productive life is a mountain.

When you exercise your faith in the word through prayer in the name of Jesus nothing can stand in your way or limit you successfully because of the One whom you have believed. He's the greater One who promised he will never leave you forsaken (See 1 John 4: 4 & 5: 4; Matthew 28: 20). This is how victory over spiritual stronghold was gained for you at the cross of Calvary and this makes Jesus your standard for living. The very reason you are to manifest the life and power from Him through you to the rest of the world by exercising the power of prayer.

The Bible enjoins you to put on Christ without whom you can do nothing [Romans 12: 2, 13: 14]. Your calling as an ambassador of the king is to adequately represent him here on earth above all things, by allowing him live his life through you to demonstrate the character of his Spirit to the rest of the world. This is your ultimate calling and the purpose is to proselytize that Jesus Christ is the Son of God, and have him formed in everyone. So they can think, say, and do that which will bring righteousness and holiness as standard for living. This is why Apostle Paul, with all that God used him to do, could still cry out saying,

> *"That I may know Him, and the power of His resurrection"* (Philippians 3: 10).

This reveals where the believer's heart should be, to desire more of his glory and presence:

15And Moses went up the mountain and a cloud covered the mountain. 16And the glory of the Lord God abode upon Mount Sinai and the cloud covered it six days: and the seventh day God called unto Moses out of the midst of the cloud. 17And the sight of the glory of God was like devouring fire on the top of the mountain in the eyes of the children of Israel. 18And Moses went into the midst of the cloud, and got up into the mountain: and Moses was in the mountain forty days and forty nights in the presence of the Lord (Exodus 24: 15 – 18).

11And the Lord spoke to Moses face to face, as a man speaks unto his friend. 12And Moses said to the Lord, see, you say to me, bring up this people, but you have not let me know whom you will send with me. Yet you said, I know you by name and you have also found favour in my sight. 13Now therefore, I pray you, if I have found favour in your sight, SHOW ME NOW YOUR WAY THAT I MAY KNOW YOU (progressively become more deeply and intimately acquainted with you, perceiving and recognising and understanding more strongly and clearly) and that I may find favour in your sight. 14And the Lord said, my presence shall go with you, and I will give you rest. 15And Moses said to the Lord, if your presence does not go with me; do not carry us up from here! 16FOR BY WHAT SHALL IT BE KNOWN THAT I AND YOUR PEOPLE HAVE FOUND FAVOUR IN YOUR SIGHT? IS IT NOT IN YOUR GOING WITH US SO THAT WE ARE DISTINGUISHED, I AND YOUR PEOPLE, FROM ALL THE OTHER PEOPLE UPON THE FACE OF THE EARTH? 17And the Lord said to Moses, I will do this thing also that you have asked, for you have found favour, loving-kindness, and mercy in my sight and I have known you personally and by name. 18And

CHUCKS UZONWANNE

MOSES SAID, I BESEECH YOU, SHOW ME YOUR
GLORY (Exodus 33: 11 – 18).

³"Grace and peace to you from God our Father and the Lord Jesus Christ, ⁴who gave Himself for our sins to rescue us from this present wicked world (evil age), according to the will, purpose and plan of our God and Father, ⁵to whom be glory forever and ever. Amen" (Galatians 1: 3- 5).

God's will and purpose is for Jesus to give himself for our sins in order to rescue us from spiritual condemnation in hell. So, Jesus declared, *"I am the way, the truth, and the life; no man comes to the Father but by me" (John 14: 6)*

The Bible says in Revelation 1: 5-6, "⁵...Unto Him that loved us, and washed us from our sins in his own blood. ⁶And hath made us kings and priests unto God and his father..." (See also Galatians 1: 4; 1 Peter 2: 24; 1 John 2: 2).

The Bible also says in *2 Corinthians 5: 21, "For He had made him to be seen for us, who knew no sin; that we might be made the righteousness of God in Him." (See also 1 Peter 2: 22, 24; 1 John 3: 5).*

1 John 3: 8 says, *"...For this purpose the son of God was manifested (appeared), that he might destroy the works of the devil."*

The Bible further reiterates in Acts 10: 38 *"How God anointed Jesus of Nazareth with the Holy Spirit and with power, who went about doing good, and healing all that were oppressed of the devil, for God was with him."*

All these scriptures makes you God's special creation patterned after Christ Jesus, chosen and empowered to be like him.

When you look at the word of God, the progressive revelation of the person of God from Genesis to Revelation, it reveals the immutable foundation upon which moral concepts such as God's grace, his love, mercy and faithfulness are based. This also reveals that you have been empowered in the name of Jesus to pull down strong holds; to cast down imaginations and everything that tries to take the place of God in your life.

"³For though we walk in the flesh, we do not war after the flesh [live according to the dictates of the flesh; human level of seeing things; our senses]: ⁴For the weapons of our warfare are not carnal, but mighty through God to the pulling down of strong holds; ⁵Casting down imaginations, and every high thing that exalts itself against the knowledge of God, and bringing into captivity every thought to the obedience of Christ..." (2 Corinthians 10: 3-5) Emphasis mine.

When you pray in the name of Jesus, you must have faith in God and speak forth by the power of prayer. This is the very reason Peter boldly speaking in the face of opposition said to the Jews and leaders of the Pharisees, *"And his name through faith in his name had made this man strong, whom you see and know; yea, the faith which is by Jesus has given the impotent man this perfect healing in the presence of you all" (Acts 3: 16).*

Having knowledge of God's word and rightly applying the word empowers the believer to change hopeless situations and live in victory. This is because there is power in prayer rendered in the name of our Lord Jesus; and this is the believer's authority over all the power of the enemy.

The Bible says in *Luke 10: 19, "Behold, I give unto you power to tread on serpents and scorpions, and over all the power of the enemy; and nothing shall by any means hurt you."(See also Mark 16: 18; Acts 28: 3- 5)*

Through prayer, speaking forth in the name of Jesus enables the believer to take authority over seen and unforeseen circumstances. With the word of God rightly confessed the believer can do exploits when he believes and prays in faith.

I am here to let you know; you can change any hopeless situation and conditions that have kept you bound. The case of the woman with the issue of blood should inspire you to pray and put your faith to action (Matthew 9: 21 – 22; Mark 5: 25 – 32; Luke

8: 43 - 48); the case of the 38 year old impotent man at the pool of Bethesda should kick-start your faith to change your confessions and speak right words in faith (John 5: 1 – 8). The case of blind Bathemaus should also awaken you to pray relentlessly without ceasing until you receive answers to your prayers (Mark 10: 46 – 52). This is your wake-up call to a new prayer life, the prayer of faith empowered by the power of prayer. This is your long awaited moment to pray relentlessly and without ceasing known as the "Now" moment. The "Now" moment is a moment between you and God to wrestle in prayer and prevail because it is yours for the taking. Go ahead and take what belongs to you in the name of Jesus as you decree that Divine health is yours, Long life is yours, Victory belongs to you in Christ, Success is yours, and greatness is yours! Go ahead and exercise your belief in prayer through faith in the word and possess your possessions.

> *"Jesus answered and said unto them, verily I say unto you, if you have faith, and doubt not, you shall not only do this which is done to the fig tree, but also if you shall say to this mountain be removed and cast into the sea; it shall be done. And all things, whatsoever you shall ask for in prayer, believing you shall receive them" (Matthew 21: 21 – 22).*

²Now there is at Jerusalem by the sheep market a pool, which is called in the Hebrew tongue Bethesda, having five porches. ³In these lay a great multitude of impotent folk, of blind, halt, withered, waiting for the moving of the water [the moving of the water signifies the Spirit of the word]. ⁴For an angel went down at a certain season into the pool, and troubled the water [stirred the water, there was an atmosphere for the miraculous]: whosoever then first after the troubling of the water stepped in was made whole of whatsoever disease he had. ⁵And a certain man was there, which

had an infirmity for thirty eight years. ⁶When Jesus saw him lie there in his condition, and knew that he had been NOW a long time in that case, he saith unto him, Will thou be made whole? ⁷The impotent man answered him, Sir, I have no man [no faith], when the water is troubled, to put me into the pool: but while I am coming, another step down before me. ⁸JESUS SAID UNTO HIM, RISE, TAKE UP THY BED, AND WALK. ⁹AND IMMEDIATELY THE MAN WAS MADE WHOLE, AND TOOK UP HIS BED, AND WALKED: and on the same day was the Sabbath (John 5: 2- 9).

The graciousness of God is revealed in you now regardless of your situation or condition. As a matter of fact, what God looks for when he looks at you is your faith and his word working in you through salvation in the name of Jesus. This enables him to perform his promises concerning you. Observing the previewed scripture, you would realise that there were great multitude of sick, infirmed and diseased folk who were waiting for the moving of the water, but the down side to their condition was that they had no faith for their healing when the water of the Spirit was stirred with the atmosphere for the miraculous. This made Jesus' compassion go out to one of them who regardless of his hopeless and negative confessions got his healing as the Lord Jesus asked him to take up his bed and go home, pronouncing him healed by faith in his spoken word. And immediately, the man was made whole and took up his bed and walked. Perhaps, your condition is such that you are impotent, blind, halt or withered waiting for the moving of the water. Whatever your situation or condition; I need you to know your inevitable victory is within you and lies in your prayer and your faith in the spoken word of God. This is because there is power in prayer through faith in the word of God.

PRAYER EXERCISE

1. Name 2 things prayer enables the believer to do? See page 238 - 244

_____

_____

2. What is the 'Now' moment? See page 243

_____

_____

_____

3. What does God look for when he looks at you? See page 244

_____

_____

_____

_____

CHAPTER TWENTY-ONE

PRAY UNTIL SOMETHING HAPPENS

⁶Do not be anxious about anything, but in everything
by prayer and petition, with thanksgiving, present
your requests to God (Philippians 4: 6).

The scripture in consideration positions the believer with caution to know much cannot be achieved without prayer. The believer is enjoined to pray in every circumstance with definite requests until he receive answers to his prayer. Prayer dispels anything and everything that tries to rob the believer of his rights and take his attention away from God. This is why every believer must be careful to rightly apply prayer in everything for appropriate decision and results. For instance, when a woman is in labour and about to give birth; there comes a time when her water breaks and labour worries set in, all that is left will be for her to PUSH and keep on pushing until the baby comes out. If for any reason she does not have the strength to PUSH, there is a tendency she might have a still birth. It matters how you PUSH when you're labouring because that determines what you are going to give birth to.

¹²"Do not be afraid, Daniel. Since the first day that
you set your mind to gain understanding and to humble

yourself before your God in prayer and fasting, your words were heard, and I have come in response to them" (Daniel 10: 12).

This verse says not to be afraid, God hears your prayers and he responds to them. You just have to be careful to know that when your prayer is delayed, it is not denied.

[14]When they came to the other disciples, they saw a large crowd around them and the teachers of the law arguing with them. [15]As soon as all the people saw Jesus; they were overwhelmed with wonder and ran to greet Him. [16]"What are you arguing with them about?" Jesus asked. [17]A man in the crowd answered, "Teacher, I brought you my son, who is possessed by a spirit that has robbed him of speech. [18]Whenever it seizes him, it throws him to the ground. He foams at the mouth, gnashes his teeth and becomes rigid. I asked your disciples to drive out the spirit, but they could not." [19]"O unbelieving generation," Jesus replied, "how long shall I stay with you? How long shall I put up with you? Bring the boy to me." [20]So they brought the boy. When the evil spirit saw Jesus, it immediately threw the boy into a convulsion. He fell to the ground and rolled around, foaming at the mouth. [21]Jesus asked the boy's father, "How long has he been like this?" "From childhood," he answered. [22]"It has often thrown him into fire or water to kill him. But if you can do anything, take pity on us and help us." [23]" 'if you can believe'?" said Jesus. "Everything is possible for him who believes." [24]Immediately the boy's father exclaimed, "I do believe; help me overcome my unbelief!" [25]When Jesus saw that a crowd was running to the scene, he rebuked the evil spirit. "You deaf and dumb spirit," He said, "I command you, come out of him and never enter him again."

26 The spirit shrieked, convulsed him violently and came out. The boy looked so much like a corpse that many said, "He's dead." 27 But Jesus took him by the hand and lifted him to his feet, and he stood up. 28 After Jesus had gone indoors, His disciples asked Him privately, "Why couldn't we drive the evil spirit out of the boy?" 29 He replied, "This kind can come out only by prayer" (Mark 9: 14-29).

The Lord Jesus lets us know it is only by prayer that certain kinds of issues and situations can be overcome. For example, a boxer who goes into the boxing ring on the day of his tournament for the first time to start his training exercise before his bout will have himself to blame if he comes out alive. He may not be able to recount his experience and may never step into the boxing ring the rest of his life.

You don't become a champion in a day, a champion is known for all the years of quality training and preparedness undergone before going into the ring to face a fierce opponent. The disciples of Jesus asked him, *"Why couldn't we drive out the demon spirit out of the boy?"* Jesus replied, *"This kind can only come out by prayer and fasting"* Signifying the importance of prayer. Another example is a soldier in training may not understand the reason for all the drill he undergoes until he is on the battle field, only then would he appreciate all the years of his pushing to keep fit. With the knowledge to stay fit, assemble a rifle, shoot a gun, evade his enemies, endure hunger and be tactical instinctively tells him what to do in a hostile environment because he has been trained for such an endeavour. The disciples of Jesus could not cast out the evil spirit in the boy because of their lack of prayer; no wonder they lacked faith and were unbelieving!

The believer's prayer life will determine what result he would expect because without hunger for regular and effective prayer, he may not be able to accomplish much and there may not be enough fire to motivate others. That he has hunger for prayer, and prays effectively also will be dependent on the level of training he got and if he paid attention to his training. A walk with God must deserve a regular hunger to pray at all times else one would not see beyond the fog. Prayer fuels your hope and gives you strength to see solution beyond challenges. With constant, fervent and everyday prayer the believer is assured and can hold on to the promises of God.

> *"But we will give ourselves continually to prayer and to the ministry of the word" (Acts 6: 1 - 4).*

The lesson here is for every child of God to use what they have and their positions positively for a just cause, knowing you have been consecrated and are in a covenant with God. When you commit yourself to God, it follows that your life will be transformed to reflect your dedication in a way that would inspire others to follow God's calling. Bearing this in mind, you must know that with prayer you can create a positive atmosphere in a hostile environment by bringing healing to the sick and hurting, peace into the life of an individual and their home, and restore love and joy in chaotic situations. I believe our society can be sanitized and be a better place if everyone would earnestly and continually pray. Prayer is a solution to a lot of challenges many people are facing today if only they will realize it and pray. You must learn to pray and keep on praying until you see a positive change in whatever you are praying about. This lets you know that no matter what the present circumstance, you must believe in the existence of God; that he hears and is willing to answer your prayer when you pray earnestly to him. The Bible lets us know that it is only *when the clouds are full of rain that they empty themselves upon the earth (Ecclesiastes 11: 3).*

You must keep on praying until your prayers saturate the heavens. If you want your prayer life to be effective and heard by

God, then you must eschew wickedness and purge your heart of sin. No one who walks in sin with evil in his heart should expect an answer to his prayer because God is righteous and holy, and cannot hear abominable prayers. Knowing he is going to visit evil doers with the rod of his judgement and so the Bible strictly enjoins everyone to repent of their sin and wicked ways and follow God through Jesus Christ.

> *"If my people who are called by my name will humble themselves and pray, and seek my face, and turn from their wicked ways; then will I hear from heaven, and will forgive their sin, and will heal their land" (2 Chronicles 7: 14).*

God already called you his people, but he also wants you to humble yourself by turning away from your wicked ways, and seek his face in truth and in spirit. It is when you're humbled that you can pray righteous prayer then would he hear and forgive your sin and heal your land.

The scripture reveals that; it is not every prayer that God answers. God cannot answer a wicked and abominable prayer because he is holy and righteous, and so he expects everyone who desires a relationship with him to be holy and walk in righteousness in Christ Jesus. The Bible lets us know the need for effective prayer in Ephesians 6: 10- 18:

> *[10]"Finally, be strong in the Lord and in His mighty power. [11]Put on the whole armour of God so that you can take your stand against the devil's schemes. [12]For our struggle is not against flesh and blood, but against the rulers, against the authorities, against the powers of this dark world and against spiritual forces of evil in the heavenly realms. [13]Therefore put on the full armour of*

God, so that when the day of evil comes, you may be able to stand your ground, and after you have done everything, to stand. [14] Stand firm then, with the belt of truth buckled around your waist, with the breastplate of righteousness in place, [15] and with your feet fitted with the readiness that comes from the gospel of peace. [16] In addition to all this; take up the shield of faith, with which you can extinguish all the flaming arrows of the evil one. [17] Take the helmet of salvation and the sword of the Spirit which is the word of God. [18] And pray in the Spirit on all occasions with all kinds of prayers and requests. With this in mind, be alert and always keep on praying for all the saints."

The scripture we just read lets us know you have been empowered through your union with God, to draw your strength from him. That strength, which his boundless might provides, is the armour of the prayer of faith with which you can ably stand against the schemes of the enemy when the day of evil comes. This is why you must be alert and always keep on praying, knowing your contention is not against flesh and blood, but against territorial powers in heavenly realms.

The Bible goes on to tell us the things you need to be strong in the Lord:

- *Truth*
- *Righteousness*
- *The gospel of peace*
- *The shield of faith,*
- *And the word of God*

With these you're further enjoined to pray all kinds of prayer and make requests in the Spirit on all occasions.

Another revelation of why you must keep on praying until something happens can be found in 2 Corinthians 10: 3 – 5:

> [3] *"For though we live in the world, we do not wage war as the world does.* [4] *The weapons we fight with are not the weapons of the world. On the contrary, they have divine power to demolish strongholds.* [5] *We demolish arguments and every pretension that sets itself up against the knowledge of God and we take captive every thought to make it obedient to Christ."*

The scripture we just read is instructive and explicit. They reveal what strategy you are to apply and bring to your understanding what you are contending against. Letting you know that the foremost thing you need are the things which were recounted earlier on, which are: *Truth, Righteousness, the word of God and the shield of faith which is prayer.* All of these things are what you need to contend successfully against wicked spirits in the supernatural sphere because your prayer strategy is not comprehensible by human standards. This is the advantage that you have of God when you pray regularly in the name of Jesus with all kinds of requests in the spirit because you are not using mere human weapons. The weapons of your strategy should be prayer at all times which cannot be understood from the human point of view, but you know they are mighty before God for the overthrow and destruction of strongholds. This is the reason you must refute arguments and human reasoning and everything that sets itself up against the truth of God's word and lead every thought to obey the word of God. Evidently, Prayer inspires your faith and creates the belief that the word of God is prevalent in all circumstances. This is the exact reason God instructed Joshua saying:

> [1] *After the death of Moses the servant of the Lord, the Lord said to Joshua son Nun, Moses servant:* [2] *"Moses my*

CHUCKS UZONWANNE

servant is dead. Now then, you and all these people, get ready to cross the Jordan river into the land I am about to give to them — to the Israelites. ³I will give you every place where you set your foot, as I promised Moses. ⁴Your territory will extend from the desert to Lebanon, and from the great river, the Euphrates — all the Hittite country — to the Great Sea on the west. ⁵No one will be able to stand up against you all the days of your life. As I was with Moses, so I will be with you; I will never leave you nor forsake you. ⁶"Be strong and courageous, because you will lead these people to inherit the land I swore to their forefathers to give them. ⁷Be strong and very courageous. Be careful to obey all the law my servant Moses gave you; do not turn from it to the right or to the left, that you may be successful wherever you go. ⁸Do not let this Book of the law depart from your mouth; meditate on it day and night, so that you may be careful to do everything written in it. Then you will be prosperous and successful. ⁹Have I not commanded you? Be strong and courageous. Do not be terrified; do not be discouraged, for the Lord your God will be with you wherever you go."

What more shall we say regarding the scripture we have just read; God gave Joshua a condition on which he will be with him as he was with Moses; some of which are for Joshua to:

- *Be strong and courageous*
- *Be careful to obey all the law Moses gave you*
- *Do not let this Book of the law depart from your mouth; meditate on it day and night*

If you carefully under-study the highlights in 2 Corinthians chapter 10, you will notice they are almost similar in meaning. *For instance, to meditate on the word of God day and night, God is simply saying to Joshua, prayer is what you need to obey the law and do everything written in it.*

We already know that Prayer is a major key in our walk with God. That with prayer you can change hopeless situations and open the doors of your destiny. With prayer you can unlock heaven's storehouse to gain victory and dominion over all the works of the enemy. Jesus started with prayer and ended with prayer; even while on the cross he still prayed. And so you cannot over-emphasis that prayer is what you need to change hopeless situations.

- Ask Daniel and he will tell you how God shut the mouth of lions when he was thrown into the lion's den (See Daniel 6: 1 – 22).
- Ask Esther and she will tell you that it was through prayer and fasting that she obtained favour with king Ahasuerus (Xerxes) (See Esther 4: 1 – 17).
- I assure you that Peter would tell you how he escaped the clutches of Herod when he was put in prison; that it was the prayer of the saints and the angel of the Lord that saved him (See Acts 12: 1 – 12). You can also ask him what he was doing on the roof top when he had a vision and went with the three men sent by Cornelius the centurion (See Acts 10: 9 – 20).
- You can ask Abraham why he prayed for Abimelech when God closed the womb of every female in his household (See Genesis 20: 1 – 7).
- Ask Paul what he was doing at sea when their ship was being tossed by the boisterous wind before they found themselves in the island of Malta (See Acts 27: 9 – 26).
- Solomon's prayer in the book of 2 Chronicles 6: 18 – 21, and God's answer in 2 Chronicles 7: 11 – 17 reveals a great deal and must re-kindle the fire of your prayer life to pray until something happens.

CHUCKS UZONWANNE

Evidently, Paul's entire epistle prove he was a man of prayer, and our Lord Jesus Christ undeniably lived a life of prayer at all times because the Bible bore witness of these in Matthew 14: 23,

> "And when he had sent the multitude away, He went up into a mountain to pray: and when the evening was come, He was there alone." "Then Jesus went with His disciples to a place called Gethsemane, and He said to them, "Sit here while I go over there and pray" (Matthew 26: 36).

> [39] "Jesus went out as usual; as was His habit to the Mount of Olives, and His disciples followed Him. [40] On reaching the place, He said to them, "Pray that you will not fall into temptation." 41 He withdrew about a stone's throw from them and knelt down and prayed" (Luke 22: 39 – 41).
>
> And James tells us to [16] "pray for each other so that you may be healed. The prayer of a righteous man is powerful and effective. [17] Elijah was a man just like us. He prayed earnestly that it would not rain, and it did not rain on the land for three and a half years. [18] Again he prayed, and the heavens gave rain, and the earth produced its crops (James 5: 16 -18).

My brother, I know the situation you are in is not an easy one! My sister, I cannot but agree the sickness in your body is overwhelming, but, I have come to encourage you irrespective of the state you are in to keep praying until something happens. Yes! Push my brother, push, and push; push my sister, keep on pushing until something happens. Your change is on the way, coming with all the promises of God. Although it may tarry, if you don't give up but keep on pushing, your victory will surely come to pass.

CHAPTER TWENTY-TWO

TESTIMONY OF A WOMAN HEALED OF FIBROID AN EQUIVILENT OF NINE MONTHS PREGNANCY

T his testimony I owe to Almighty God whose pre-eminence is unquestionable, to Pastor Chucks that man of prayer whose delight is to demonstrate the character of the Holy Spirit. Who desires to see men healed of infirmities and free from the clutches of darkness. To all those who prayerfully and relentlessly stood in the gap for me, and last but not the least, to the doctor who further encouraged and inspired my faith and assured me of his specialty in his chosen field. Indeed, he is a specialist who knows his salt, a believer and a praying child of God at that.

My story began to unfold when I first visited the hospital. At my first consult, I was told I had a grown fibroid equivalent of nine months pregnancy. It was with mix feeling that I left the hospital not knowing what to do. All sorts of thoughts were racing through my mind, but somehow I found the peace of God and the strength to be resolute and put my trust in God through prayer.

This strength within me from God kept me going even though I knew a lot was taking place inside of me. This testimony is about what God has done in my life and I know and believe that he can do much more in your own life if you will trust in him whole heartedly and seek him prayerfully.

With prayer, God delivered me from what would have been my demise. Compounding the situation was the fear I knew as a result of people I know who have lost their dear loved ones to fibroid. News from out of town regarding prominent celebrities who met their untimely death due to this uncanny growth that spreads like wild fire; coupled with the fear inspired by the first consultant I met gave me serious food for thought. These made me have a rethink about my priorities in life. I was going through an indescribable excruciating pain especially during my menstrual periods. It was such that on one occasion I passed out for some split seconds and regained consciousness almost immediately. That was the first miracle I experienced with God as I sought his face for a solution. I have kept my ordeal to myself praying only to God and asking for his intervention and at a point I thought to only mention to my immediate younger sister my condition whom I asked to prayerfully keep it to herself pending when all issues with the consultant was finalised. As the days went by I noticed my tummy was growing bigger and bigger and on the increase with pain. Life was being drained out of me by this agent of darkness, yet I would go to work everyday to do my chores. People thought I was pregnant but deep within me I would pray and cry to God to have mercy and heal me. Year in, year out, the pain increased with every inch of growth my body put on, my clothes became undersized and I made up my mind to see another consultant without further delay. The first consultation particularly was not encouraging at all. He was negative and full of death. His confessions instilled fear and death; nevertheless, I refused to accept his testimony and insisted I consult with a different doctor.

An appointment was later arranged for me to meet with another consultant after three months that seemed like eternity.

And so, I began to prepare my mind in anticipation for a positive deliberation with the second consultant and also to know how soon the operation will take place because at this time I was getting beside myself with pain.

Prior to my next visit to the hospital, I informed, Pastor Chucks the senior pastor of Christ House of Destiny Ministries who drew up a programme for me on days to pray and fast. I had organised to meet with some of my siblings at the prayer meeting perhaps if anything happened during the operation, I would have seen them to reassure them that it was alright if it's the Lord's wish for me.

On this faithful prayer day, Pastor Chucks called down heaven as we all began to pray, the atmosphere was transfigured and electrifying. The presence of God was very strong and felt by all as Pastor Chucks began to pray and prophesy. After praying and anointing me with oil, he prayed for all those who were present and said to me, 'Oyinye, hear what the Spirit of the Lord is saying, 'your operation will be successful and you will be in the hospital ward for just one week and you will be discharged and your recovery and healing will be so rapid that anyone who sees you and hears of your predicament will marvel and give glory to God.' And by the leading of the Spirit, he said several other beautiful things about those who were present. It so happened that when I consulted with the second consultant at the same hospital where the first doctor was all negative; the second consultant reassured me all was going to be well. That the operation was going to be successful. And indeed, the operation was successful with about seven doctors involved, over nine hours operation and over fifty-five fibroids were removed. As prophesised, I was in the hospital for only seven days according to the word of the Lord, glory be to God. With my ordeal and experience, I now realise the value and importance of life much more than before; that there is more to

CHUCKS UZONWANNE

life than all the things we crave for. It made me to have a deeper understanding and awareness that life is a gift from God and must be lived in the worship and reverence to God and love for all humanity. As a Christian, God has used my situation to prove to me that there is indeed power in prayer and that he is the prayer answering God. I bless the Lord for all he has done for me. For taking away pain from my life, sorrow from my family and healing me according to his word. Thank you Lord Jesus - Oyinye.

CHAPTER TWENTY-THREE

ALL KINDS OF PRAYER

May the Lord God bless you and keep your lamp burning, and may he keep you strong to the end.

May his countenance shine providence on you always, you being fruitful and productive?

May the Lord keep you standing where standing is not easy, and may you be fulfilled for all to see your life reflect the glory of God as he opens the door of your destiny for you to walk in your greatness and success?

I pray for the wholeness, completeness, abundance, and divine peace of God to rest upon you and mantle you totally and continually in the mighty name of our Lord and Saviour, Jesus Christ. Amen.

PRAYER FOR YOU!

I pray in the name of Jesus that God would continually birth great new things in my life, family, ministry, and every area of my endeavour.

I pray for my onward march and an upward life of grace, fresh anointing, strength, divine health, sound mind, fruitfulness, productive, greatness, success and an open door for my destiny to shine forth the glory of God always, prospering the works of my hands.

As I focus on Jesus and surrender all to follow the author, Perfecter, and finisher of my faith; I will walk and not stumble, I will run and not grow weary because the joy of the Lord will continually be my strength.

In the name of Jesus, I belong to God to will and to do of his good pleasure.

Because the grace of God is upon my life, goodness and mercy will always lead me to walk humbly in greatness and in success in the mighty name of Jesus, amen.

PRAYER OF CONFESSION

Father, I thank you for establishing me to have right standing with you and to live holy and godly life being a good ambassador of Christ worthy to be called your own.

Blessed redeemer, I thank you for sending your Son Jesus Christ to atone for my sin and to redeem me from every work of darkness.

By your grace I am free and reconciled with you to do great exploit in your name; winning souls into your kingdom by witnessing the gospel to my sphere of contact and testifying of your love.

Thank you Father! I give you all glory for empowering me with all that pertain to life and godliness as I decree that I am an overcomer; more than a conqueror because greater are you in me than he that is in the world.

I confess and declare that I have the life of God in me and the Spirit of the Son of God is at work in me to will and to do of your good pleasure, all to your glory in the mighty name of our Lord Jesus Christ, amen.

•   •   •

Father, in the name of Jesus I confess and declare that I and my family will continually abide and serve in the house of the Lord all the days of our lives.

I confess that your excellent Spirit is making tremendous power available in the life of every member of my family, granting us sound mind, assimilation and retention, Spiritual wisdom, Revelation knowledge and enlightening the eyes of our understanding to comprehend and always know our hope in Christ Jesus.

O Lord God, I stand on your word as I confess and decree that sickness, infirmity and diseases are far from us; poverty and lack will not come near our dwelling in the name of Jesus.

I confess and decree that increase, productiveness and prosperity are ours in Christ Jesus. I confess that divine health, strength and long life belong to us always in the mighty name of Jesus Christ, amen.

PRAYER OF APPRECIATION

Father, we are gathered as the family of Christ in your holy presence and our hearts and minds are open to be instructed, healed and spiritually imparted; to be illuminated, transformed and to receive from you:

- A heart of Christ
- A heart of love
- Spiritual wisdom
- Revelation knowledge
- Strength
- Divine health
- Sound mind (comprehension, assimilation; retention)
- Grace for increase; dominion in every area of our lives; to subdue and bear good fruits all to your glory, in the name of Jesus. Amen.

PRAYER OF CONSECRATION

Father, in the name of Jesus, I ask for the birthing of a consecrated life.

May your word invigorate and transform me that I be led by your Spirit always to walk in spiritual wisdom and in revelation knowledge; clothed with grace and in righteousness.

I ask that your word from my mouth reflect who you are always and be a blessing to someone today in the mighty name of our Lord Jesus Christ, amen.

PRAYER OF EMPOWERMENT

Father, in the name of Jesus, I ask that you lead me to someone who needs your word to make a change and receive salvation. Let your word come alive and minister grace to the hearer.

As I minister your word in the name of Jesus, I stand in the authority vested in me as your anointed one and I decree for fibroid and tumour to dry up.

I decree for the barren womb to receive correction and bear fruits.

I decree for the lame to walk, the blind to see and for deaf ears to hear.

Let your word bring healing in every area of the lives of the needy today in the mighty name of Jesus, amen.

PRAYER FOR THE SICK

I pray in the name of Jehovah Rapha for the healing of the sick and for sinners to be saved in the mighty name of our Lord Jesus Christ. Amen.

• • •

Father, I pray in the name of Jesus, thanking you that your word from my mouth is spirit and alive to bring healing to the sick and to all nations. As I pray for the sick; I speak forth words with power in the name of Jesus, and by the authority vested in me; I command every fowl spirit and every power of darkness to lose their grip over the life of these ones. I pray that burdens be removed and yokes destroyed in the mighty name of our Lord Jesus Christ.

I pray that everyone under my influence who are sick, infirmed and diseased; receive their healing and be made every wit whole in the name of Jesus. I decree that your word O Lord God has the ability to reproduce life and restore divine health to as many as believe. Therefore, I stand on your word because your word will not return until it has accomplished the purpose for which it has been spoken forth for in the mighty name of Jesus.

I pray O Lord in the name of Jesus that every fibre of their being, every marrow of their bones, their joints and blood; from the crown of their head to the souls of their feet and the tips of their toes to receive strength and correction through the quickening and healing blood of our Lord and Saviour Jesus Christ, amen.

Scriptures for meditation

Isaiah 55: 11	Matthew 21: 21-22
James 5: 13-15	Mark 5: 22-29
Mark 9: 14-29	Matthew 9: 1-8

PRAYER FOR FAMILY

Father, in the name of Jesus, I pray that by your grace my family is endowed with wisdom for the upward life as we flourish and bear good fruits always.

Thank you Holy Spirit; for helping my family to be focused and to be exemplary in our walk with you; to the intent that everyone who comes in contact with us sees your mighty work in us.

Thank you King of Glory, as a family we're strengthened with might in our inner-man by your Spirit to live in strength and perpetual health.

Thank you for granting us sound mind and renewing our youth as we sower like the eagle; and for ordering our footsteps and establishing the works of our hands as we preach the gospel of peace.

O Lord God, I thank you; for your love and peace that permeates our spirits, our souls, our body, and our home; and for establishing our relationship with men that they may be drawn to you in holy reverence.

Father, we pray that you continually open the door of increase in our life and in our home as you crown our efforts with all that pertain to life and godliness. That as our life reflect who you are, men everywhere will give their hearts to you for salvation that they may know you.

Thank you, for you are our Lord and Shepherd, the glory and the lifter up of our head, and the joy of our salvation.

Thank you for prospering and establishing the work of our hands with greatness and with success, in the mighty name of our Lord Jesus Christ, amen.

Scriptures for meditation

Acts 10: 2	Ephesians 5: 1-2
Isaiah 32: 17	1 Thessalonians 3: 12
Romans 7: 4	Colossians 1: 10-11
3 John 2	1Timothy 3: 15

PRAYER OF GUIDANCE

Father, what a privilege it is to be in your presence today; for the seed of your word to be planted in my heart and mind.

Thank you Holy Spirit for covering me with your glory; as I sit at your feet to be taught in the way of righteousness I ask O Lord for a transformation; that I may know you and the power of your resurrection.

Thank you for hearing and empowering me to walk in victory and dominion, in strength and in divine health as I receive soundness of mind and grace for increase in every area of my life.

•   •   •

Father, I thank you for your banner over me is love! Holy Spirit, I welcome you as I stir the water of the atmosphere of the miraculous.

I ask that you take pre-eminence and fill my heart with your love and presence, in the name of our Lord Jesus Christ. Amen.

Thank you for I am in your presence once again to be refreshed and covered with your glory; for the eyes of my understanding to be enlightened as I gain spiritual wisdom, revelation knowledge, grace for increase, and for causing me to be fruitful and productive.

I pray oh God that your word will mantle my heart and mind to think the right thoughts and walk in your righteousness. Thank you Holy Spirit for I am daily loaded with strength to do great and uncommon things unto the glory of God the Father as I walk in victory and dominion, in every area of my life in the mighty name of our Lord Jesus Christ. Amen.

•   •   •

Father, in your holy name I present myself to be taught, to be instructed, counselled on the inside and spiritually imparted.

CHUCKS UZONWANNE

My heart and mind are open to receive from you the word of life.

Illuminate my heart and mind with heavenly verities and grant me comprehension with sound mind to receive and retain your word for the impartation and transformation of my world in the name of our Lord Jesus Christ, Amen.

• • •

Father, I pray as I walk with you today that you will enlighten my darkness.

Bring me to the place of peace, joy and love. Unveil my eyes to see what you see and my heart to think thoughts that will bring you glory and honour.

Thank you for ordering my footsteps; for leading me unto victory and dominion.

Thank you for prospering the works of mine hands; making me great and successful and a blessing to my world, in the mighty name of Jesus, amen.

PRAYER OF MEDITATION

I'm a child of God born of God's Spirit, and I'm privileged with grace to be in the presence of God always. Therefore, Father I thank you, for hearing and answering me. In the name of Jesus, I ask for the seed of your word to be planted in my heart that I bear good fruit unto your glory always.

Holy Spirit, I thank you for inundating me with your glorious presence as I meditate on your word of life. I ask for a spirit, soul and body transformation that I may know you and the power of your resurrection.

Thank you for empowering me with strength and perception to walk in victory and in dominion, in sound mind and in divine health. I receive all that pertain to life and godliness; grace for increase in every area of my life. And I pray oh Father, for the healing of the sick and for sinners to be saved all to your glory in Jesus mighty name, amen.

PRAYER OF THANKSGIVING

Father I thank you, for I am covered with your Holy Spirit and your glory! I am grateful for your word has taken root in my spirit, and by your Holy Spirit, I am continually led to walk in victory and in dominion, in strength and in divine health.

Thank you Lord Jesus for peace in my life, for granting me sound mind; and grace for increase as I prosper and bear good fruit in every area of my life.

King of glory! I thank you for hearing and granting my request; meeting every of my need, in the mighty name of our Lord Jesus Christ. Amen.

CHRIST HOUSE OF DESTINY MINISTRIES

Voice of Bliss Outreach International
London, United Kingdom.

Tel: +44 (0)750 8230 404, +44 (0)740 4984 650

Email: christhouseofdestiny@yahoo.co.uk
            christhouseofdestiny@gmail.com
Website: www.pastorchucks.com
            www.christhouseofdestiny.com

Join us on face book follow us on twitter Visit us on You Tube

Books By Pastor Chucks Uzonwanne

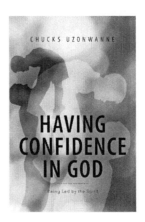

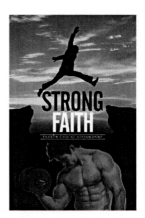

Other Books By Pastor Chucks
Faith versus Prayer   Godly Perspective
The Elevation of the Spirit   The Seed of Faith

Available At:
KICC & Good News; Dominion Centre & City Gates. And many Christian & Online bookstores
Website: www.pastorchucks.com www.amazon.com www.xlibrispublishing.co.uk
www.barnesandnoble.com

Christ House of Destiny Ministries, London United Kingdom.
Tel: +44 (0)75 0823 0404 Email: christhouseofdestiny@yahoo.co.uk
Join us on face book. Follow us on Twitter. Visit us on U Tube